Simple Guide to Safer SAILING and BOATING

ARCO PUBLISHING COMPANY, INC.
219 Park Avenue South, New York, N.Y. 10003

Published 1974 by Arco Publishing Company, Inc.
219 Park Avenue South, New York, N.Y. 10003

Original title: *The Skipper's Course*

ISBN 0-668-03412-2 (Paper Edition)
ISBN 0-668-03502-1 (Library Edition)
Printed in the United States of America

TABLE OF CONTENTS

INTRODUCTION

THIS is a self-instructional program and might be a little different from most books that you're used to. Here's how it works. Each page is called a frame. In a frame, we will ask you to read and absorb a fairly small amount of information. Then, to make sure you've learned and remember it, we'll stop and ask you to answer some questions. When you have done this, we will tell you right away whether or not you were right. If you gave any wrong answers be sure to review the material before continuing. You can work at your own pace and may stop anytime for a break. Now, find a comfortable, well-lighted, and quiet place to work. Then turn the page and begin.

PART I, PRELUDE TO BOATING

A. Overview

1. So you're going to be a Skipper? Then welcome to the group of some of the nicest people you'll ever meet. In the past few years, recreational boating has undergone an enormous growth in the number of boats on the water and the number of people who participate (recently estimated at more than 40 million). Our waterways are becoming crowded in many areas. There *are* dangers and hazards for ignorant and careless people. To protect such people, and innocent bystanders, the Federal government, the states, and some communities have laws and regulations designed to keep recreational boating a safe sport. Much of what you need to learn is based on these *legal requirements*. The program begins with this subject. Do not try to go too far at first. You may take a break anytime. Each topic is immediately followed by a QUICK QUIZ so that you can see how well you are learning. Be careful to compare your answers with those given on the following pages. In this way you will complete the program at your own speed and with full success.

B. Classes of Boats

2. Remember back when you were responsible for your first car? If you do, you'll recall that your first concern might well have been the legal requirements. That is, the registration certificate, number plates, and possible inspection for all safety equipment. With boats it is very nearly the same thing. Your first concern is the legal requirements. There are both Federal and state requirements. The state requirements vary from state to state. We will cover only the Federal requirements.

Many of the things that you must do and the types and amount of equipment you must carry on your boat are determined by one simple factor, the CLASS of your boat. The class is determined by the overall boat length. Shown below is a sketch of a small, open, outboard motorboat.

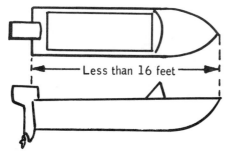

As you can see the outboard motor is NOT included in the measurement. If a boat (like the one shown in the sketch) is less than 16 feet it is said to be a class A boat. The equipment required for a class A boat will differ from that of other classes of boats. If the overall length of this boat is between *16 feet* but less than *26 feet* it is a class 1 boat. As before, the overall length is taken from the tip of the bow in a straight line to the back (stern) of the boat.

This is a sketch of an open-day cruiser.

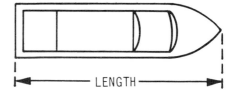

The next sketch is an outline of an auxiliary sailboat with an engine and sails. This sketch was chosen to give you examples of attachments *not* included in the overall length to determine class.

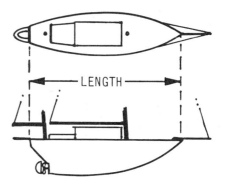

If this boat's overall length is between 26 and 40 feet, it is a class 2 boat. The short piece of spar attached to the bow, the bowsprit, and the attachment on the stern with the odd name of boomkin are not included in the overall length.

When the overall length of a boat is between 40 and 65 feet, it is a class 3 boat.

You will need to remember the four classes of motorboats, how a class is determined, and the lengths for each class. To help you remember, fill in the table below.

Class __A__ = less than _____ feet.
Class __3__ = _____ feet to less than _____ feet.
Class __1__ = _____ feet to less than _____ feet.
Class __2__ = _____ feet to _____ feet.

Try these questions without looking back.

1. Motorboats are divided into _____ classes.

2. The classes of motorboats are:

    _____
    _____
    _____
    _____

3. What is the only determining factor for the class of a motorboat?

4. List all the classes of motorboats and their determining factor.
    Class_____is less than ___ feet.
    Class_____is ___ feet to less than ___ feet.
    Class_____is ___ feet to less than ___ feet.
    Class_____is ___ feet to _____ feet.

5. Shown below are some familiar sketches of boats with different lengths. Using the lengths, fill the class of each boat in the appropriate blanks.

    a.   = Class___

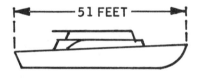

    b.   = Class___

    c.   = Class___

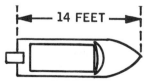

d.   = Class___

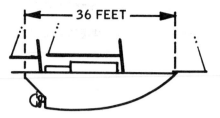

C. Legal Requirements

1. Numbering.

The rule for numbering boats is quite simple. Any boat that is capable of being mechanically propelled must be numbered. A motorboat is numbered for the same reason that your car is numbered — to identify it. Boats are registered and numbered in much the same manner that a car is registered. Once the proper forms are obtained from your state agency, fill out and return with the appropriate fee. A certificate of number will be received. These numbers must be put on the bow of your boat in a certain way. For example, suppose you were from the state of Michigan. Your assigned number might look like this:

MC 9912 CF

These numbers and letters must be painted or permanently attached to the forward part of your boat close to the bow. They must be in block characters, in a color that contrasts with the background, and not less than *three* inches in height. Paint or mount them on both sides of the bow so that they look like this:

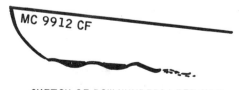

SKETCH OF BOW NUMBERS LEFT SIDE

2

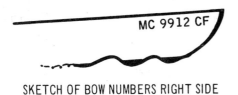

SKETCH OF BOW NUMBERS RIGHT SIDE

Make sure you leave a space between the first letters and the numbers that follow as well as between the numbers and the last letters. The space should be about the size of the letter "M." Don't try to use fancy lettering like this:

UNACCEPTABLE LETTERING

It's too hard to read and will not be accepted by either the Coast Guard or state boating officials. You will also receive a small wallet-sized card which is your Certificate of Number. Don't forget to carry it or have it in the boat anytime you are using the boat. That's the first thing the Coast Guard Boating Safety Detachment will want to see.

If you sell or transfer your boat you have to turn in your certificate of numbers. If the boat is going to remain in use in the same state, the same number is issued to the new owner.

QUICK QUIZ: (Numbering) (answers on page 4)

1. Here is an imaginary boat number:

    AN8934AC

    Print these numbers on both the right and left side of the bow of the boat shown below the way you think it should be done.

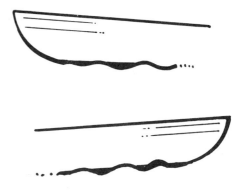

2. Shown below is a sketch of a boat. This boat must be numbered.

    True ☐   False ☐

3. If you are ever stopped and boarded by a Coast Guard Boating Safety Detachment what is the first thing they will want to see?

    Write your answers here

    _____

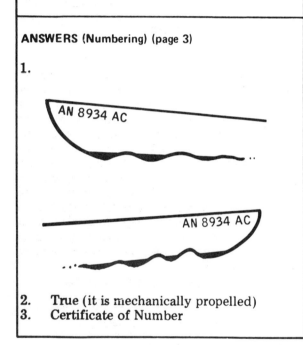
2. Equipment

OK, then . . . the first thing to do is to get the boat properly numbered. Next you'll need to furnish the boat with the proper equipment so that it can legally operate on the water. The law requires certain *minimum* equipment in the boat. That equipment depends upon the class of your boat. Let's consider each piece of equipment individually.

Back-fire Flame Arrester

If your boat has a gasoline INBOARD or INBOARD-OUTBOARD engine, it must be equipped with an acceptable means of back-fire flame control. This usually means that you will need a Coast Guard approved flame arrester on the carburetor. If you have an OUTBOARD engine, a flame arrester is not required.

THIS MIGHT HAPPEN WITHOUT THE FLAME ARRESTER

BACK FIRE FLAME ARRESTER

Personal Flotation Devices (PFD)

It is important that you understand the definition of a Personal Flotation Device. There are many things which may be used as general life-saving devices in emergencies. Perhaps a good example of one would be the beverage cooler which some skippers carry in their boats. The important difference between these and PFD's is that a Personal Flotation Device is designed to keep an *individual* afloat in the event of (you should pardon the expression) an emergency.

I STILL SAY WE SHOULD'VE WORN PFD's.

The next important point to learn is that the Coast Guard *does not* approve of all PFD's. Federal law sets the highest manufacturing and performance standards. These must be met before the Coast Guard will approve a PFD for use in boating. OK — how do you tell if the PFD's you've chosen have been approved by the Coast Guard? It's easy. All PFD's approved by the Coast Guard have that approval stamped on the PFD or on an attached tag.

All boats, regardless of class, must carry ONE PFD for each person in the boat, including any water skiers, even though they might be under tow. Boats less than 16' in length can carry any approved PFD for every person aboard. Boats 16' or longer must carry a type I, II, or III for each person on board and one type IV for the boat to provide man overboard protection. The chart below explains the types.

All Coast Guard approved life preservers manufactured today are colored a bright, highly visible, Indian-orange shade. A life preserver is a type I and should not be confused

with what we call a "buoyant vest" [type II]. Buoyant vests may be any color. They also have less flotation material than life preservers. The approved PFDs often will be marked for the following sizes: ADULT, CHILD MEDIUM, and CHILD SMALL. This means that you should pick out and buy PFDs for your boat with the same care you would use in selecting a mink coat for your wife or girlfriend.

Readiness for Use

Give this requirement a lot of thought. Although your PFD's should be kept where they won't get kicked around or abused, they must be readily *accessible* when you and any guests are in the boat. Of course, when the boat is *not* in use, they should be stowed in a dry, well-ventilated place. Before getting underway, bring them out where they can be grabbed in an instant. If you are ever boarded by a Coast Guard Boating Safety Detachment for examination and they find that your PFD's aren't quickly accessible, you may receive a citation (ticket). The reason we place

PERSONAL FLOTATION DEVICE TYPE NUMBER	BRIEF DESCRIPTION OF THE DEVICE	THOSE BOATS ON WHICH THE DEVICE WOULD BE ACCEPTABLE BY THE COAST GUARD
TYPE I	LIFE PRESERVER WITH MORE THAN 20 POUNDS OF BUOYANCY, AND DESIGNED TO TURN AN UNCONSCIOUS PERSON FACE-UP	ALL RECREATIONAL BOATS
TYPE II	BUOYANT VEST WITH AT LEAST 15.5 POUNDS OF BUOYANCY AND DESIGNED TO TURN AN UNCONSCIOUS PERSON FROM A FACE-DOWN TO A FACE-UP FLOATING POSITION	ALL RECREATIONAL BOATS
TYPE III	BUOYANT VEST OR JACKET WITH AT LEAST 15.5 POUNDS OF BUOYANCY. NOT DESIGNED TO TURN AN UNCONSCIOUS PERSON FACE UP	ALL RECREATIONAL BOATS
TYPE IV	A THROWABLE DEVICE SUCH AS THE RING BUOY OR THE FAMILIAR BUOYANT CUSHION	ACCEPTABLE AS PRIMARY LIFESAVING EQUIPMENT ON RECREATIONAL BOATS LESS THAN 16 FEET IN LENGTH.

so much importance on the requirement for having your PFD's ready and available is this: of the hundreds of drownings caused by boating accidents, in many of the cases *a PFD was available but was not used!* Here's an idea that works pretty good. Make your PFD's really personal by stenciling the names of your family on them. For example: on yours, stencil "Captain" or "Skipper" and your name, then for the wife, stencil "Mate" and her name, and for the kids (if any), "Crew" and their names. Next, get all hands to put them on and adjust the straps and fasteners for each individual and leave them that way. Now your PFD's will be ready for each wearer. Finally, a lot of those people who drowned were Skippers who were apparently too proud, too foolish, or too something to put on their PFD when they should have.

"THAT'S ACCESSIBLE???"

RING LIFE BUOY

Ring Life Buoys [TYPE IV]

Many boaters include a ring life buoy such as the one shown in the illustration above as part of their lifesaving equipment. These devices are especially handy for tossing to persons in the water. As you can see, they have grab ropes and a line so that the ring buoy can be hauled in after it has been thrown out. Make sure your ring buoy is also Coast Guard approved. All Coast Guard approved ring buoys are either white or orange. Attach approximately 60 feet of line to the grab line and mount the ring buoy on brackets where it will be readily accessible. When throwing it in the water, be careful not to hit the person with it. If your boat is 16 feet or longer, your must carry one type IV device.

CUSHION

Buoyant Cushions [TYPE IV]

Buoyant cushions, such as the one shown in the illustration, serve the dual role of boat seat cushions and lifesaving devices. Since you sit on them, they are handy in an emergency, and they are easy to throw to a person in distress. However, they do not provide good protection for children, nonswimmers, and injured persons because they must be held. When using them, grasp the straps or put your arms through the straps and hug the cushion to your chest. *Never wear the cushion on your back like a pack since it will turn your face under water.* Any cushion used should bear the Coast Guard approval. Also, since they receive rougher treatment than other lifesaving devices and, as a result, wear out faster, inspect them frequently for tears in the plastic envelope and for broken straps.

Who is to Wear

This is not always an easy question for you to answer because it involves a personal judgment on your part. First, *all* small children should wear a PFD in the boat at all times. Small children are almost always active and like to climb around exploring. Second, *all* nonswimmers, both children and adults, should wear a PFD in the boat. Third, if you have any passengers or guests who might be physically handicapped, see that they also wear a PFD in the boat.

When to Wear

Again, this is a judgment situation. In general, however, whenever the weather worsens from anything but clear and calm — then *all* hands get into a PFD. In areas of heavy boating traffic or when you're taking the boat through choppy water such as the mouth of a river or a tidewater inlet, put them on. Professional mariners, Coast Guardsmen, and all Old Salts will get into a PFD at the drop of a hat. (That's how they got to be an OLD Salt.) Make sure your PFD's are ready to be worn. Fit and adjust the straps and fasteners for each individual before you leave the dock or launch area. Leave the fasteners unhooked to eliminate that step when time is critical.

Stowage and Care of PFD's

Most PFD's will last a long time if you give them reasonable care. Don't put them away wet. Stow them in a dry, well-ventilated place where they can be grabbed quickly if you need them in a hurry. Every now and then, air and dry them in the sun. Before you put them away, check for tears and broken, or torn, straps. *Get rid of* a damaged PFD and replace it with an approved one. Before you leave the dock or a launching ramp get every child and nonswimmer into a PFD. A number of people have drowned needlessly because a PFD wasn't available — or (even worse) if it was, it wasn't used. Don't forget — you're the Skipper and you set the rules.

Never allow a PFD to be used as a cushion unless it was meant to be. Nor should you permit them to be used as a bumper, fender, or as a toy. Make sure all adjustable straps have been set to the size of the person who might have to wear it before you leave the dock or ramp. The Coast Guard does it, the Navy and Merchant Marine both do it — why shouldn't you do it? Hold an occasional drill with the PFD's in the boat. Get your people used to getting their PFD out and on quickly.

QUICK QUIZ: (PFD's) (answers on page 10)

1. The color of Coast Guard approved life preservers is _____

2. The buoyant vest although approved by the Coast Guard has less _____ than the life preserver.

3. If you're throwing a ring life buoy to a person in the water, be careful not to
   _____

4. If you're in the water with a buoyant cushion, *never* wear it on your _____

5. You can tell it's an approved PFD by the
   _____

6. All boats must carry at least one PFD for every person in the boat including _____

7. PFD's should be worn at all times in the boat by _____ and _____

8. When out in your boat keep your PFD's readily _____

Ventilation

The greatest cause of fire and explosions aboard recreational boats is gasoline fumes (vapor) collecting in the low parts of the boat (bilges). Gasoline vapor is heavier than air and sinks to the lower compartments. If a flow of clean air isn't present to blow gas vapor out of the boat then it sits there waiting for the first spark — from a cigarette ash — an electric switch — and . . . Think about this for a moment, one cup (one-half pint) of gasoline allowed to vaporize has the same explosive power as FIFTEEN STICKS OF DYNAMITE. It doesn't take a lot of imagination to picture what effect that power would have exploding in the bilges of a 25-foot cabin cruiser.

No completely foolproof ventilation system has yet been developed. However, some form of adequate ventilation is required by law.

Fresh air is ducted into low spaces using wind scoops (cowls). Large flexible tubes lead down to the areas to be ventilated from the wind scoops. A similar tube leads to the exhaust cowl where the collected vapor is vented safely overboard. The flexible tubes connecting the low areas with the intake and exhaust cowls should be at least 2 inches in diameter. Shown on next page is a sketch of a typical outboard motorboat ventilation system with a fixed fuel tank.

Note that the intake cowl faces forward to scoop in the air and force it into the compartment. The exhaust cowl faces aft; the wind blowing over it creates a slight vacuum,

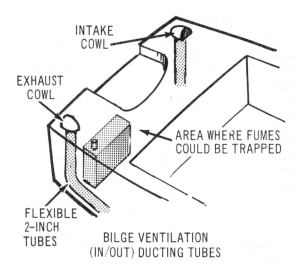

INTAKE COWL

EXHAUST COWL

AREA WHERE FUMES COULD BE TRAPPED

FLEXIBLE 2-INCH TUBES

BILGE VENTILATION (IN/OUT) DUCTING TUBES

helping to draw out any accumulated vapors. REMEMBER this system only works well when the boat is going forward or when there is a breeze blowing from ahead.

Now study the sketch below. This is a second method for forcing air into the engine and fuel-tank compartments. The wind-activated rotary exhauster head, similar to a cowl, is on the cabin roof. The intake cowl on the side of the boat forces air into the boat and the rotary exhauster head draws it out. Again this system depends on forward motion of the boat or a good breeze.

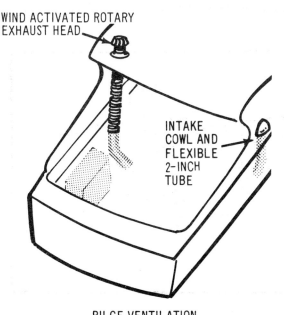

WIND ACTIVATED ROTARY EXHAUST HEAD

INTAKE COWL AND FLEXIBLE 2-INCH TUBE

BILGE VENTILATION
(Wind activated rotary exhauster head)

Special vapor and explosion-proof electric fans can also be used. If you choose a powered blower make sure you select a spark-proof electric switch to turn it on.

LIGHT'S OKAY... HOW'S YOUR VENTILATION?

QUICK QUIZ: (Ventilation) (answers on page 10)

1. Gasoline is most dangerous when it turns into a _____

2. The best way to prevent danger from fuel vapor is to have adequate _____

3. A well-ducted ventilation system will have at least one _____ duct and one _____ duct.

4. Gasoline in boats is always a safety hazard because the vapor is _____ than air.

5. An electric blower for ventilation should be _____ proof.

Signaling Devices (Sound)

There will be times when you will need to make loud sound signals. For example, in periods of low visibility, fog, mist, heavy rain, etc., you are required to make proper signals with either a horn, whistle, or a bell. Although the equipment laws do not require a Class A boat to carry these, a Class A boat must still make the proper sound signals when maneuvering and in low visibility to comply with other requirements. Shown below are sketches of audible noise-making devices that are suitable and easy to carry on Class A boats.

A Class 1 boat does not have to carry a bell, but it must have a horn or whistle aboard. It can be the kind that is operated by hand, mouth, or power. It must be loud

ANSWERS TO QUICK QUIZ: (PFD's) (page 8)

1. Orange or indian orange
2. Flotation (material)
3. Hit them
4. Back
5. Words "USCG Approved"
6. Water skiers
7. Children — nonswimmers
8. Accessible

ANSWERS (Ventilation) (page 9)

1. Vapor
2. Ventilation
3. Intake-exhaust (in either order)
4. Heavier
5. Flame or explosion (either word)

YES if required and NO if not required; add asterisk(s) where applicable (see below).

QUICK QUIZ (Sound) (answers on page 12)

	Class A	Class 1	Class 2	Class 3
Bell				
Whistle/Horn				

* Must be power operated

** Although not required, must still sound proper Rules of the Road signals.

Fire Extinguishers

I know that I need fire extinguishing equipment, but what type and how many? The answer to this question is again based on boat class and Federal requirements. On boats with permanently installed, approved fixed-fire extinguishing systems, the required number of portable hand-operated fire extinguishers is less. For that matter, Class A and Class 1 boats with fixed fire extinguishing systems in engine spaces do not need any portable units to meet minimum requirements.

Approved fire extinguishers are identified by letter and Roman numeral according to the type of fire they are designed to put out and their size. Extinguishers approved for motorboats are hand portable, for either the B-I or B-II classification.

Extinguishing agents that are approved by the Coast Guard are listed in the table below. This table also points out the relationship of the Roman numerals to the amount (size) of extinguishing agent. It is important to note at this time that toxic vaporizing — liquid-type extinguishers, such as those containing carbon tetrachloride of chlorobromomethane are not approved and are not accepted as required fire extinguishers because their vapors are harmful when inhaled.

enough to be heard at least one-half mile. Shown below are examples of devices that will meet that requirement.

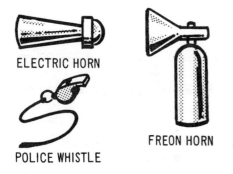

ELECTRIC HORN

POLICE WHISTLE

FREON HORN

Class 2 and 3 boats must carry a bell, and a whistle or horn that can be heard for *one mile.* On Class 2 boats the whistle or horn can be either hand or power operated. Class 3 boats must carry a power-operated horn or whistle. Shown below is a blank table for boat classes and applicable horn/bell requirements. To help you remember these requirements, see if you can complete the table without referring back to the text. When you have done so, check your table with ours and write

FIRE EXTINGUISHERS

Class (type-size)	FOAM (Min Gals)	CARBON DIOXIDE (Min Pounds)	DRY CHEMICAL (Min Pounds)	FREON (Min Pounds)
B-I	1¼	4	2	2½
B-II	2½	15	10	—

Now, how can you be sure that the extinguisher you have purchased or are about to purchase meets Coast Guard approval? It's easy enough — just look at the label. Fire extinguishers manufactured after 1 January 1965 will be marked (for example) "Marine Type USCG Type *B* Size *I* Approval No. 162-028/EX . . . " Shown below are typical examples of fire extinguishers that have been approved for motorboats.

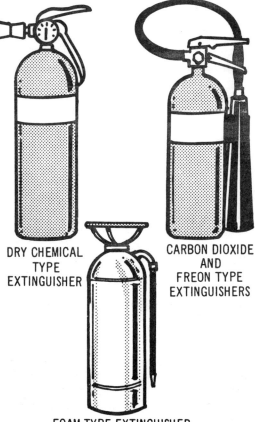

DRY CHEMICAL TYPE EXTINGUISHER

CARBON DIOXIDE AND FREON TYPE EXTINGUISHERS

FOAM TYPE EXTINGUISHER

Now let's go back and find out the full story on just how many fire extinguishers are required on your boat.

On Class A and Class 1 outboard motorboats, that do *NOT* carry passengers for hire or are constructed so that explosive or flammable gases cannot be trapped in low spots, do not require fire extinguishers. It's true — they're not, but why take a chance? You've heard the story many times before about an ounce of prevention — and this is one ounce **of prevention that could really pay off. One approved B-I-type, hand-portable fire extin-**

guisher is required on motorboats less than 26-feet in length when passengers are carried for hire or the boat has spaces that can trap explosive gases or vapors. The sketch below illustrates areas where gases can be trapped on outboard motorboats.

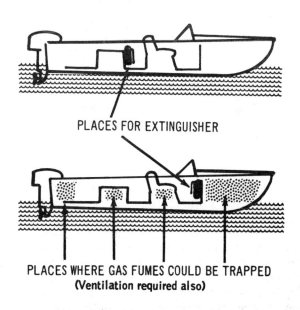

PLACES FOR EXTINGUISHER

PLACES WHERE GAS FUMES COULD BE TRAPPED
(Ventilation required also)

Does your boat have one or more of these areas? If so, make sure you carry at least one fire extinguisher. To sum up the requirements study the table on page 12 for a moment.

FIRE EXTINGUISHER REQUIREMENTS

Minimum Number of Hand-Portable Fire Extinguishers

Class of Boat	When no fixed fire extinguishing system in engine space	When a fixed fire extinguishing system is installed in engine space
A	One B-I	None
1	One B-I	None
2	Two B-I or one B-II	One B-1
3	Three B-1 or one B-I and one B-II	Two B-I or one B-II

You now know what type and how many fire extinguishers are required, so what else is there? Several things, such as where they should be located, how they should be cared for, and how they are used.

Suppose you store your fire extinguisher in the bow storage compartment. In this location a very agile person could probably retrieve it in 2 or 3 minutes. In that time your boat and your life could be lost. Check your extinguishers, are they located where they are easy to grab?

Make frequent checks to be sure your extinguishers are in their proper stowage brackets and undamaged. A cracked or broken hose should be replaced, and nozzles should be kept free of obstructions. Extinguishers having pressure gauges should show pressure within the designated limits. Locking pins and sealing wires should be checked to make sure that the extinguisher has not been used since last recharged. Extinguishers should never be tried just to see if they are in proper operating condition. The valve might not reseat and result in a slow leak. A discharged extinguisher should be recharged right away!

QUICK QUIZ: (Fire Extinguishers) (answers page 14)

1. This is a sketch of a 24-foot, open-day cruiser with an inboard gasoline engine and permanent fuel tanks installed. It does *not* have a fixed fire extinguishing system installed.

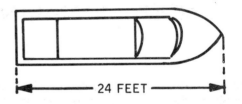

What type and how many fire extinguishers does this boat require? If you need to, refer to the table on page 12. Your answer: _____ of type

_____ .

2. Shown below is an open outboard runabout 14-feet in length with a closed fuel compartment.

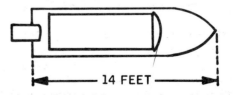

What type and how many fire extinguishers does this boat require?
Your answer: _____ of type _____ .

SHALL I TRY TO PUT IT OUT OR KEEP SIGNALING FOR HELP?

3. Shown below is a sketch of a 50-foot cabin cruiser with a fixed fire extinguishing system installed in the machinery spaces.

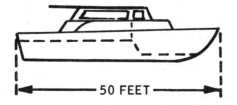

What type and how many hand-portable fire extinguishers does this boat require?
Your answer: _____ of type _____ or _____ of type _____ .

4. Shown below is a sketch of a 35-foot auxilliary sailboat. It is powered by sails and a small inboard engine without a fixed fire-extinguishing system in the engine space.

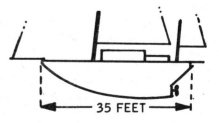

What type and how many portable fire extinguishers does this boat require?
Your answer: _____ of type _____ or _____ of type _____ .

13

speeds. The trailer must be hooked up in such a way that no part of the boat or trailer (except the hitch) can contact your car during a maximum turn. The safety chains should be installed as shown in the diagram below, with enough slack to allow for maximum turns. Too much slack and the chains will drag; too little and sharp turns will be hampered.

RECOMMENDED METHOD FOR
ATTACHING SAFETY CHAINS

D. Safe Boat Trailering

Many boat owners at one time or another will be required to trailer their boat. Before jumping off, however, you will need some knowledge of trailer safety and practices.

The fit of boat to trailer is very important. The trailer should be about the same length and width as your boat, and it must be rated to handle the total boat and equipment weight. Trailer rollers should be adjustable to fit the hull, and tie-downs must be provided to hold down your boat when it is on the trailer. The winch and its line must be heavy enough to launch and reload without breaking. A power winch (if used) should be capable of manual operation.

OK, let's hook up the trailer and hitch. Frame-mounted hitches are your best bet. They are superior to the bumper hitch because swaying and fishtailing (a common occurrence with a bumper hitch) are reduced at high

Your hitch load should be balanced and all parts should be checked for tightness and proper operation. Next, the tires on the trailer and the car should be correctly inflated. Low-tire inflation pressure on one side or both sides of the trailer will cause it to rock and roll from side to side. Low pressure in rear tires of the car could cause the trailer to bottom over rough roads.

A well-balanced trailer will not cause the rear end of your car to sag. A trailer is well balanced when the coupler weight can be handled easily by the average man.

Have your trailer wheel bearings been greased recently? Submerging in water when loading and unloading washes out grease very

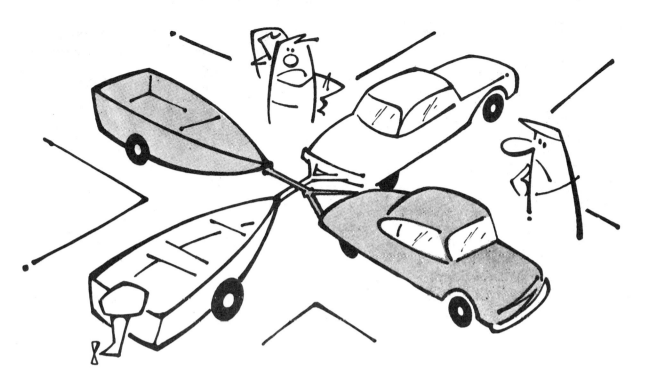

rapidly and will cause bearings to burn out. Wheel bearings should be repacked at least twice a year or each time they are submerged in water.

Be sure your lights, brakes, and trailer registration meet the requirements of all the states in which you will be traveling.

E. Review, Part I, Prelude to Boating

In this first part of the "Skippers Course" you learned the *classes* of recreational boats. This topic was first since Federal requirements are based on the class of a boat. You'll recall that the only factor in determining the class of a boat is its overall length. We have asked you to identify the class of a boat, given its length.

The next topic was numbering your boat and how to properly put them on your boat. Don't forget to carry your certificate of number with you whenever you're in the boat.

The subject of required safety equipment was next. Again we wish to emphasize this is the *legal minimum* that is required. Boats with *inboard gasoline* engines must have an acceptable means of backfire flame control.

Personal Flotation Devices was the next and may be regarded as one of the most important topics to learn. This was followed by the ventilation requirements and the required fire extinguishers. The required noise makers

(bells, horns, and whistles) were discussed, ending with the topic of safe boat trailering. There are several boating books and pamphlets available which you can send for that cover these subjects in more detail. Refer to Appendix 2 for information where these texts can be obtained.

The table below summarizes the legal minimum required equipment which we have presented in more detail in this part of the program.

Minimum Required Equipment

EQUIPMENT	CLASS A (Less than 16 feet)	CLASS 1 (16 feet to less than 26 feet)	CLASS 2 (26 feet to less than 40 feet)	CLASS 3 (40 feet to not more than 65 feet)
BACK-FIRE FLAME ARRESTER	One approved device on each carburetor of all gasoline engines installed after April 25, 1940, except outboard motors.			
VENTILATION	At least two ventilator ducts fitted with cowls or their equivalent for the purpose of properly and efficiently ventilating the bilges of every engine and fuel-tank compartment of boats constructed or decked over after April 25, 1940, using gasoline or other fuel of a flashpoint less than 110°F.			
BELL	None.*	None.*	One, which when struck, produces a clear, bell-like tone of full round characteristics.	
DEVICES ***	One approved life preserver, buoyant vest, ring buoy, special purpose water safety buoyant device, or buoyant cushion for each person on board or being towed on water skis, etc.			One approved life preserver or ring buoy for each person on board.
WHISTLE	None.*	One hand, mouth, or power operated, audible at least ½ mile.	One hand or power operated, audible at least 1 mile.	One power operated, audible at least 1 mile.
FIRE EXTINGUISHER—PORTABLE When NO fixed fire extinguishing system is installed in machinery space(s).	At least One B–I type approved hand portable fire extinguisher. (Not required on outboard motorboat less than 26 feet in length and not carrying passengers for hire if the construction of such motorboats will not permit the entrapment of explosive or flammable gases or vapors.)		At least Two B–I type approved hand portable fire extinguishers; OR At least One B–II type approved hand portable fire extinguisher.	At least Three B–I type approved hand portable fire extinguishers; OR At least One B–I type Plus One B–II type approved hand portable fire extinguisher.
When fixed fire extinguishing system is installed in machinery space(s).	None.	None.	At least One B–I type approved hand portable fire extinguisher.	At least Two B–I type approved hand portable fire extinguishers; OR At least One B–II type approved hand portable fire extinguisher.
	Fire extinguishers manufactured after 1 January 1965 will be marked, "Marine Type USCG Type —— Size —— Approval No. 162.028/EX . . ." **			

*NOTE.—Not required by the Motorboat Act of 1940; however, the "Rules of the Road" require these vessels to sound proper signals.

**NOTE.—Toxic vaporizing-liquid type fire extinguishers, such as those containing carbon tetrachloride or chlorobromomethane, are not accepted as required approved extinguishers on uninspected vessels (private pleasure craft).

***WIth few exceptions, all boats (not just motorboats) are required to carry PFD's.

QUICK QUIZ: (Review)

To test yourself on how well you have mastered this part of the program, see how you can solve the following problem:

Suppose that you are a boarding officer of the U.S. Coast Guard. You are about to board the 36-foot cabin cruiser in the sketch shown below. You are going to inspect this boat for all legal requirements. This boat is powered by two gasoline inboard engines and does not have a permanently installed fire extinguishing system aboard. The Skipper has five guests aboard. What is the minimum required equipment you would be inspecting for? If you need to, use the table and the sketch but try to answer without it. List your answers here — then check them with the ones given on page 18.

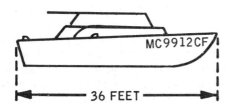

———————————————————
———————————————————
———————————————————
———————————————————
———————————————————
———————————————————
———————————————————
———————————————————
———————————————————
———————————————————
———————————————————
———————————————————
———————————————————
———————————————————
———————————————————
———————————————————
———————————————————
———————————————————
———————————————————

PART II, SAFETY AFLOAT

A. Presailing Procedures

1. What About the Weather?

As the Skipper, weather is going to be a primary concern of yours. Things like — what is the weather where I want to take the boat? Not only *now* but what is it expected to be in 6 to 8 hours?

Since the very first step in planning a boating trip is to check the weather and weather forecasts, you must know some of the weather data sources.

1. *Local Newspapers.* Read the whole report not just the summary. A good idea is to tear the report out of the paper and take it with you. Make sure it applies to the waters you're going to boat in.
2. *The Telephone.* The National Weather Service publishes Coastal Warning Facilities Charts for all coastal areas plus the Great Lakes. The location and phone numbers of all National Weather Service offices plus the location and times of AM and FM radio and television marine weather broadcasts are listed also. Finally, the first page of your local telephone directory lists the number to dial that will connect you to a recorded weather forecast that is periodically updated.
3. *Special Radio Sources.* Coast Guard stations broadcast weather on 2670 kHz. These broadcasts are preceded by an announcement on 2182 kHz. If you have a radiotelephone aboard,

you can also call the marine operator for weather. The National Weather Service broadcasts continuous marine weather on the radio frequency 162.55 MHz (VHF/FM). Most of these broadcasts, however, are only made in coastal areas.

4. *Special Warnings and Storm Signals.* At many marinas, launching ramps, yacht clubs, and Coast Guard stations, storm warnings are displayed by flag hoists or lights. As the Skipper, you must know the meaning of each of these hoists and lights.

When you see this bright red pennant (daytime) flying from a storm signal flagpole it means that winds of up to 38 miles per hour are expected over the local water area. With these winds there can be waves, rough water, and white caps (sprays). It is called a "SMALL CRAFT ADVISORY" and the meaning to you is — STAY ASHORE! If your boat is tied up or moored, check all mooring lines and double them if necessary. Close all ports, hatches, and doors. Make sure your mooring cover (if used) is tightly fastened. At night the small craft warning is one red light over a white light and means the same thing — winds up to 38 miles per hour.

"IT LOOKS LIKE THE SIGNAL FOR HURRICANE..."

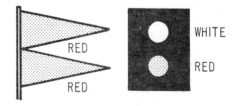

This signal displayed on a mast means GALE winds up to 54 miles per hour. At night this warning is displayed by a white light at the top with a red light below. The meaning of this signal to you, Skipper, is, if *possible*, get your boat out of the water, or if not possible, tie it up with extra lines.

"DON'T WORRY — IT'LL PROBABLY PASS RIGHT OVER US."

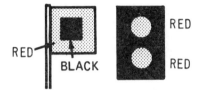

When you see this signal it means STORM with winds up to 72 miles per hour. Your boat should be out of the water and under shelter, if possible, and you should be home checking flashlights, candles, and storm drains. At night two red lights, one over the other are displayed and have the same meaning.

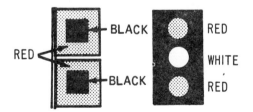

Finally, when you see this signal (and we hope you never will) it means HURRICANE with winds 72 miles per hour and up. For you, Skipper, do the same things as with the signal for STORM only with more vigor. At night (if the pole is still standing) the signal is *three* lights. Red at the top, white in the middle, and red at the bottom.

The table below summarizes the storm signal system.

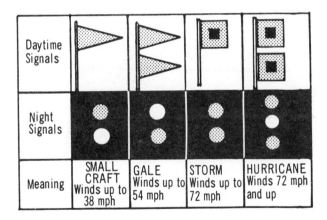

Daytime Signals				
Night Signals				
Meaning	SMALL CRAFT Winds up to 38 mph	GALE Winds up to 54 mph	STORM Winds up to 72 mph	HURRICANE Winds 72 mph and up

Don't ignore a small craft advisory. A fool and his boat are soon parted. Remember too, you can get into very bad weather conditions even with a fair forecast. Line squalls, thunderstorms and the like are very unpredictable and therefore very dangerous to small craft. As the Skipper, you alone have the responsibility for the safety of your boat and its passengers. Keep an eye on the weather, make the right decisions about going in to shelter and stick to them.

18

QUICK QUIZ: (Weather) (answers on page 20)

1. List at least three pre-sailing sources of weather information.

2. List at least two radio weather information sources underway:

3. List the meaning of the flag and light displays shown below.

STORM SIGNALS

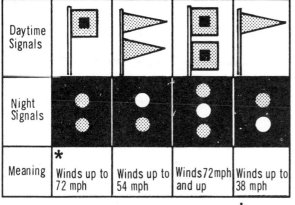

Daytime Signals				
Night Signals				
Meaning	*Winds up to 72 mph	Winds up to 54 mph	Winds 72mph and up	Winds up to 38 mph

ENTER THE MEANING OF EACH SIGNAL HERE *

B. The Launching Ramp

If you're the kind of Skipper who likes to boat in different waters or you don't moor the boat to a pier or mooring, you'll be continually launching the boat from a trailer, usually down a hardtop ramp. Often this is done in front of a highly critical audience and, of course, you don't want to look like a greenhorn. There are some things to do and some not to do if you want to look like an "Old Pro."

1. *Ready to launch.* Park well clear of the ramp area. *Everyone* out of the car and *nobody* in the boat! Cast off the boat holddown straps or clamps and stow them in the car. Climb into the boat and make sure the drain plug is closed and tight. Make one last check for any loose gear that might slide around during launching. Now, out of the boat and check the winch. Make sure it's still in the *locked* position. Tilt the engine or outdrive unit to the *up* position so that it won't strike the ramp. Finally, and just to make sure, (if you have a tilt type trailer) check the tilt lock and safety chain to see that the tilt is still *locked.* OK — ready to launch?

2. *Launching.* Again, everybody *out* of the boat. Station one person to give you any needed directions as you back the boat and trailer to the water. Back down slowly (this is no time to make a panic stop) until the stern of the boat is in deep enough water to float free when it is pushed off the trailer. Stop the car, set the emergency brake and turn off the engine. Attach a bow line to the boat and have someone hold the line. Unlock the tilt latch and its safety chain (if you have one). Unlock the winch and cast off the winch line hook. Push the boat off the trailer into the water. If you've kept the rollers properly lubricated, the boat will move off the trailer easily.

3. *Clear the ramp.* Remember other boatmen may be waiting to launch so drive your car and trailer to a parking space as soon as the boat is launched. After you've parked the car make one

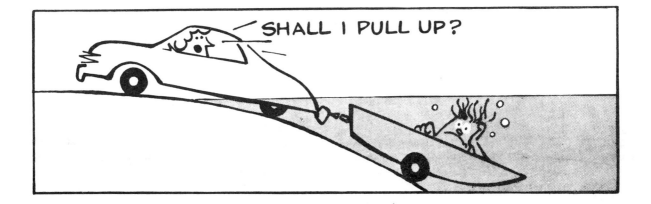

last check to see that the boat hold-down straps or clamps and winch crank handle (if removed) are in the car.

4. *Clear the boat from the launch area.* If there's a pier or float close to the launch ramp it is generally best to tie up and prepare the boat there. If not, board the boat from the ramp over the bow. The person holding the bow line should stay ashore and hold the boat until you're fully ready to start the engine.

QUICK QUIZ: (Launching) (answers on page 22)

Fill in the blanks:

1. Park the car and trailer clear of the _____ area.

2. Release and stow the _____ _____.

3. _____ person(s) in the car and _____ in the boat.

4. While backing down the ramp have _____ person(s) direct you.

5. Before you get out of the car set the _____ .

C. FUELING

You are about to toss three to five cases of dynamite, with fuses attached into your boat — you don't think so??? Well then consider this:

You'll remember one cupful of gasoline (vaporized) has the same EXPLOSIVE power as fifteen sticks of dynamite!!!!

All this means that fueling the boat should be done very carefully. A number of serious accidents occur yearly from gasoline explosions and fires. Nearly all were due to the Skipper's failure to observe simple precautions. There are five common sense rules to apply when fueling. You must *learn* them and *do* them.

1. Always fuel the boat in good light.
2. When the boat is tied up at a fueling dock:
   a. don't smoke, light matches or lighters, or operate electric switches.
   b. Stop engines, motors, fans — anything that might cause a spark.
   c. Secure all fires, galley stoves (don't forget the pilot light on gas stoves and refrigerator).
3. Before you start to fuel:
   a. Check the mooring of your boat and get everybody out of the boat.
   b. Close ports, windows, doors and hatches — (Keep the fumes and vapor out of the boat).
   c. Check your tanks, filler pipes, tank vents, and flame screens.
   d. Check to see how much fuel the tank will take.
4. During fueling:
   a. Keep the nozzle of the hose on the can in contact with opening to prevent static sparks.
   b. Guard against spillage — if fuel spills, wipe it up immediately! Don't let any vapor get below.
5. After fueling:
   a. Replace caps (covers) of fill openings.
   b. Open up the boat *completely* and ventilate.
   c. Air out the boat for *five* minutes.
   d. Give all low spots (engine bilges, tank spaces) the sniff test. If you smell gasoline vapor, continue to air out the boat — look for spillage and leaks.
   e. Wipe up all spills.

Fueling is an important operation — and you as Skipper should do it yourself. After all, no one can do it better than you — right?

QUICK QUIZ: (Fueling) (answers on page 22)

1. Fueling a boat requires:
☐ a. A high degree of skill.
☐ b. That the boat be wide open.
☐ c. A vapor detector.
☐ d. Good light.

2. Gasoline is most dangerous when:
☐ a. It is in a liquid state.
☐ b. When it evaporates and forms vapor.
☐ c. In a flexible hose line.
☐ d. In portable tanks.

3. Gasoline hose nozzles must be kept in contact with filler openings to prevent:
☐ a. Spillage
☐ b. Static electric sparks
☐ c. Vapor from forming
☐ d. Gas from reaching the engine bilges.

There once was a boatman named Dooling,
Who skylarked while completing his fueling.
The blast from that day blew Dooling away;
Dooling shouldn't've been fooling while fueling.

D. The Float Plan

There are two things you must do before you leave home to go out in your boat. We've already discussed the first one — check the weather. If you're a new skipper the second might be news to you. That is, file a "Float Plan." It's the same idea as that used by airplane pilots (most of them anyway) who file a flight plan. Here's what you do. As soon as you have planned a boating trip and have checked the weather, tell a *reliable* relative, friend, or neighbor, WHERE you're going, WHO you will have with you, and WHEN you're coming back. Please don't ask to file your float plan with the Coast Guard, we just don't have the required facilities. Stick to your float plan once you're out on the water — if you should go to another area — then your float plan is no good. When you return from your boating trip be sure to *cancel* the float plan — that is, tell those concerned that you're back. As you might have already concluded, the reason for the float plan is simply this: If you were out in your boat without filing a float plan and if anything should happen (run out of gas — run aground, or worse) no one would know where or when to come looking for you!

A sample float plan form is shown in Appendix 5. Use it as a guide when you file yours.

It is very important that you understand why the Coast Guard emphasizes the importance of the Float Plan. Filing a Float Plan with a friend or neighbor, sticking to the plan, and canceling it when you reach your destination, all are equally important but for different reasons. When you file a Float Plan and become overdue, it is known that it is time to go look for you. But if you don't stick to your plan or fail to cancel it on return the Coast Guard might have a false alarm on its hands.

This is what happens when a small craft is reported overdue to the Coast Guard Rescue Coordination Center. Here the Coast Guard uses its resources to try to confirm that a boat *is* overdue and may be in trouble. The next stage is the "Alert." In this stage Coast Guard boats and aircraft on patrol are alerted to look for the missing boat. In the last stage "Distress" extra search and rescue boats, aircraft, and even the big Coast Guard cutters could be dispatched to carry out a planned search pattern. The Coast Guard Auxiliary may also be called upon to assist. So you see, the fuel alone used in such an operation would run your boat for years. The reason is, that lives are risked (even though it's their job) and money spent.

QUICK QUIZ: (Float plan) (answer on page 24)

1. The four w's of the float plan are:
   _____ you're going.
   _____ you're going.
   _____ you're coming back.
   _____ you have with you.

E. Making Ready to Sail

Loading the Boat

As a new Skipper this can be one of the most important subjects in this learning program. Here's the problem. In an overwhelming number of cases where someone died as a result of a boating accident, the basic cause was overloading or improper loading.

A boat's stability is affected by people (and things) moving about when on board. This is especially true of boats 16 feet and under. Let's consider the three things you're likely to put in the boat that are going to affect its stability, flotation, and how it behaves underway.

First, People — the number of seats in the boat *are not* a reliable indicator of how many people you can safely carry. There are two good ways by which you can determine the number of people you can safely take in your boat. One of these is the boat manufacturer's capacity plate. Not all boats have this plate. But it looks like this:

U.S. COAST GUARD CAPACITY INFORMATION
MAXIMUM HORSE POWER
MAXIMUM PERSONS CAPACITY (POUNDS)
MAXIMUM WEIGHT CAPACITY
PERSONS MOTOR & GEAR (POUNDS)
THIS BOAT COMPLIES WITH U.S. COAST GUARD SAFETY STANDARDS IN EFFECT ON THE DATE OF CERTIFICATION
MODEL NO   SERIAL NO
MFD BY

Normally this plate is mounted in the boat by the manufacturer near the operator's position. Note that the capacity plate states the MAXIMUM number of people the boat can safely carry. BUT — it assumes that the engine is of the size recommended, that there is a *normal* amount of fuel aboard, and that *normal* amounts of equipment and supplies are aboard, AND wind, water, and weather conditions are nearly perfect. The final assumption is that the AVERAGE weight of people in the boat is 150 pounds each. That's a lot of assumptions — what it means is that YOU, the Skipper, must exercise some very careful judgment regarding how many people to take with you. *You* are still (and always) responsible.

As we said, not all boats have this capacity plate. If you have a boat that does not have a capacity plate, a small amount of simple arithmetic will provide you with a reasonable guide for the number of people your boat can safely carry. However, the arithmetic to be used is based on the same assumptions that the capacity plate are. These assumptions bear repeating. They are: the engine you have is of a size (weight and horsepower) proper for your boat's hull, that there is a normal amount of fuel, equipment,

and supplies aboard, that wind, water, and weather conditions are just about perfect, and that the average weight of the people in the boat is 150 pounds. With these conditions in mind then, the following arithmetic will give you a reasonable guide for the number of people you can take out on your boat. First, measure the overall *length* of your boat. Next, find the width at the widest part of the boat. When you have measurements which are not whole numbers of feet, express them in tenths of feet like this:

5 feet 6 inches = 5.5 feet
18 feet 9 inches =18.75 feet

Now multiply the overall length by the width of your boat as measured. Finally, *divide* the result of that multiplication by 15. The number 15 is a constant and comes from the assumption that the *average* weight of the people in the boat would be 150 pounds. We just drop the zero so that our answer will be in people, not pounds.

Example:

Suppose you had a Class 1 boat 18 feet long and 5 feet 6 inches wide. Then:

18 x 5.5 = 99
and dividing by 15 or,
99/15 = 6.6 people!

Obviously you cannot have 6 tenths of a people — so here's what you do. Round off 6.6 DOWNWARDS to the nearest whole number or in this case 6 people, and you pick up an added safety factor. For a drill, try this procedure out on *your* boat *now*. When you have done so, write the number on white tape and stick it near the operator's position on your boat as a reminder for safe loading.

More On Loading the Boat

You now have a good idea of how much you can put in your boat. Next let's talk about where and how to load the boat. Assume you've finished fueling after launching and you're tied up to a pier. Skipper, YOU get into the boat first. Step in — don't jump in. Have people on the pier hand you any gear. See that it is distributed evenly and stowed as much out of the way as possible. Any heavy gear that might slide around in the boat should be tied down or secured. A shifting load has killed more than one boatman.

When all your gear is secured in the boat, then have your passengers step into the boat *one at a time*. Although the animals went

23

QUICK QUIZ: (Loading) (answers on page 26)

1. A capacity plate when mounted in a boat:
    - ☐ a. Gives the total weight capacity of people, gear, fuel, and engine.
    - ☐ b. The weight and horsepower of the recommended engine.
    - ☐ c. The number of people and horsepower of the engine.
    - ☐ d. The number of people only, based on an average weight of 150 pounds.

2. A capacity plate, when mounted in a boat, will be located:
    - ☐ a. Near the steering wheel and throttle.
    - ☐ b. Next to the engine serial number plate.
    - ☐ c. Near the back (stern) of the boat.
    - ☐ d. On the transom next to the engine.

3. A 20-foot boat with a 6-foot beam can safely carry:
    - ☐ a. 7 people
    - ☐ b. 8 people
    - ☐ c. 9 people
    - ☐ d. 10 people

4. The primary cause of fatal accidents in boating is:
    - ☐ a. Overpowering with too large an engine.
    - ☐ b. Fire and explosions from improper fueling procedures.
    - ☐ c. Too great a speed in rough water.
    - ☐ d. Overloading or improper loading.

aboard the ark two-by-two, remember, Noah's boat was on dry land at the time. In summary: When loading a boat distribute the load evenly, and don't allow people to stand in *small* boats.

Shown on the next page are some sketches of boats that are improperly loaded.

As Skipper, whenever you have any one of the conditions shown on the next page and you're underway in your boat — first slow down, then redistribute the weight carefully to maintain proper trim. Remember these four simple rules:
1. Distribute the load evenly.
2. Keep the load low in the boat.
3. Don't stand in small boats.
4. Never overload.

Check Equipment

Now that you've loaded the boat, check to see that your safety equipment is still accessible. Some of the equipment can use a quick working check. This will only take a minute so make it a habit.

First, PFD's — are they ready to grab? Check the straps to be sure they are secure and not torn. Make sure everybody in the boat sees them and knows how to put them on. A short drill with them (passengers and PFD's) won't hurt, especially if they have never worn a PFD before.

Second, fire extinguishers — are they aboard? In the proper rack or clamp? Can

LOADING YOUR BOAT

TOO MUCH WEIGHT IN BOW

TOO MUCH WEIGHT IN STERN

TOO MUCH WEIGHT ON ONE SIDE

OVERLOADED

connected and tested? Did you remember to bring the ignition key (if used)?

Sixth, auxiliary equipment — not a legal requirement. Is the first aid kit in the boat and ready (full)? Bucket, bailer, or hand pump? Oar or paddle and boat hook? Spare propeller and shear pin (for outboard)? Anchor line and anchor? Mooring — tow lines? Flashlight (test it)? Distress flares (dry and ready to use)? For a complete list of recommended items send for a copy of CG-340, Recreational Boating Guide (see Appendix 4) and keep it in your boat box.

they be quickly removed for use? Is the clamp frozen with rust? Do your passengers know where they are and how to use them? Have you checked the pressure gauges to make sure they are fully charged and ready to use? Are the safety pins free to remove? Don't test your fire extinguishers by pressing the start lever — the valve may not reseat afterwards and all the pressure could leak out.

Third, are all fuel tanks stowed properly? Are the covers on tight? All spillage wiped up? Are the hoses connected properly to tank and engine (for outboards)? Have you checked for fuel leaks?

"I THOUGHT YOU BROUGHT THE FLASHLIGHT..."

Fourth, lights and horn. This is an easy, quick check — just try them out briefly. Spare fuses in the boat box? Spare lamps, bulbs, too? Is there a bell, plastic whistle, or hand-operated horn in the boat box in case the horn fails?

Fifth, engine — is it down and locked (for outboards)? Is it set at the proper angle for the load in the boat? Are the fuel hoses connected tightly? Are the steering cables

F. Part II Safety Afloat Review and Exercise

As before, this review and exercise is provided in order that you be able to check yourself on how well you have mastered this part of the program. We hope by now you recognize that we have tried hard not to waste your time with things that are "nice to know" about boating. The subjects to be learned are restricted to what we feel is "must know" information. We urge you, then, to complete the following review and exercise before tackling the next part of this program.

Review

In this part of the program you taught yourself the elements of presailing procedures. Things such as sources of weather information and how to use them. Then the procedures for launching the boat (important for those Skippers who trailer their boats). Next (and very important also) the procedures in fueling the boat and ventilation of dangerous fuel vapors. We closed this part with a lesson on the "Float Plan" where you learned that you should tell a relative or reliable neighbor (who can describe your boat) where you're going, when, who you have with you, and when you're coming back. — Don't forget to cancel the Float Plan when you return.

In the part on making the boat ready, you learned the factors for loading the boat, and the difference between overloading and improper loading — remember — this is still the cause of most fatal boating accidents. We then took up equipment checking, accessibility and readiness for use, finishing with PFD's.

SAFETY EQUIPMENT

Exercise, Part II Safety Afloat (answers pg. 30)

The following exercise is arranged in the format of situational problems. Read each problem carefully, then jot down your answer before you check the one given. If you look closely, you'll often find clues to the answer.

1. Charlie Noble planned to go fishing first thing in the morning (well before daylight). Upon his arrival at the marina where he kept his boat, Charlie noted that although the sky was clear and the stars could be seen, it seemed pretty breezy. The wind speed indicator at the foot of the mast showed winds of 35 miles per hour. Looking up to the mariner's weather warning mast Charlie saw a signal that confirmed his worst fears. "Oh well, Charlie said to himself, "I was supposed to mow the lawn today anyway."

Draw a sketch and describe the signal you think Charlie saw.

2. Charlie Noble and his wife Zelda decided to trailer the boat up to the lake, try the new launching ramp, and cruise the lake. Up to a point Charlie did everything right. However, as he was walking back from the parking area, he saw that Zelda was making frantic signals to hurry. "Charlie," she yelled, "The boat is sinking!" "Drat!" said Charlie, "I forgot to_____."

What do you think Charlie forgot to do?

3. Ordinarily Charlie Noble was as safe a boatman as could be. Today, however, Charlie made a mistake. It was a beautiful day but very hot at the fuel dock. Not a breath of air was stirring. During preparation and actual fueling he did everything right. When the tanks were full he tightened the covers and wiped up the small spillage immediately. As he carefully returned the fuel hose to its rack, he tossed the ignition key to Zelda saying "Here, warm up the engine while I pay for the gas."

In view of the circumstances what do you think Charlie's mistake was?

4. Charlie and Zelda planned to go boating on Lake Wet. "Zelda," Charlie said "You pack the lunch while I go over and tell Irving where we are going." Charlie's friend, Irving Plimsole, was in his home all that day to classify his wagon wheel collection. While waiting his turn at the fuel dock, Charlie overheard a group of boatmen talking about the great trip they had just returned from. The trip was up the length of Lake Wet, through the connecting river, then to Lake Dry. "That sounds like a great trip," Charlie said to himself, "I think I'll do it." and he did ... and he committed another boating boo boo!

What do you think it was? Jot down your answer here.

"WELL I THOUGHT YOU FILED THE FLOAT PLAN!

THE COAST GUARD TODAY LAUNCHED A MASSIVE SEARCH....

"ZELDA, REMIND ME IN THE MORNING TO CANCEL OUR FLOAT PLAN."

5. On the way back to the Marina Charlie and Zelda stopped at a little beach for a swim and an early supper. The beach was covered with driftwood which Charlie thought would make great firewood (and the price was right). "Hey, Zelda," he said "get in the boat and help me load a mess of this driftwood to take home for firewood." "Gadzooks," said Zelda (she had an unusual vocabulary you see) "that's a good idea Charlie." Not wanting to damage their PFD's with the wood, Zelda carefully put the PFD's in the bow cuddy. Working quickly Charlie and Zelda soon had a heaping pile of driftwood in the boat.

They committed two unpardonable sins, what were they?

_____

_____

_____

_____

_____

_____

_____

_____

1. Since it was still dark (the stars were out), what Charlie saw at the weather warning mast was two lights. A red light on top and a white light below like this:

   This signal means "Small Craft Warning — Winds to 38 MPH." — If you got this one give yourself 20 points.

2. Charlie forgot to check and secure the boat's drain plug — 20 points for this one.

3. With no breeze blowing and tied up to the fuel dock, Charlie should have aired out the boat thoroughly before telling the late Zelda Noble to start the engine. 20 points.

4. Charlie filed a Float Plan alright but he failed to stick to it — a cardinal sin in boating. 20 points for this one.

5. First, Zelda's zeal in putting the PFD's in the bow cuddy put them out of immediate reach. Second, a heaping pile of driftwood may have created an overloaded condition. Finally, a loose pile of driftwood could suddenly shift and cause the boat to capsize. This would be called improper loading — 20 points.

   A score of 100 is outstanding!!

PART III, UNDERWAY

A. Rules of Operation

1. On-the-Spot Corrections

Under the Boating Safety Act of 1971 the Coast Guard can now do something that they couldn't do before--that is, when in their judgment, they observe a boat operating with an unsafe condition (say, grossly over-loaded) and they determine the unsafe condition is especially hazardous, they can take action. That is they can "terminate" that boat's trip by directing the boat to the *nearest* dock (or safe area) and have it stay there until the condition is corrected.

2. Negligent or Grossly Negligent Operation

If a Coast Guard Boarding Officer observes a boat being operated in a negligent or grossly negligent manner (for example, pulling a water skier through a busy swimming area) this could result in a fine or jail! The difference between negligent and grossly negligent operation is a matter of knowledge or ignorance. Speeding in a zone clearly marked "5 MPH MAKE NO WAKE" could be viewed as grossly negligent and could result in either a fine, jail, or both. You are responsible for learning and observing all rules and regulations regarding the operation of your boat. The following subjects are primarily concerned with the operation of your boat — so study them carefully.

3. Accident Reporting

If you learn and practice all of the safety points in this program there's a good chance you may never have to fill out and send in an accident report. However, some other boat *could* run into you. In this case you might have to fill out an accident report. This is required by law. There are three conditions that require you to fill out and send in a boating accident report. These are:
1. When a life is lost due to the accident.
2. When someone is injured and incapacitated (laid up) for 24 hours or more.
3. Damage of more than $100 to property (including boats).

If these seem general to you, remember it's best to file a report if you have any doubt. If anyone died you *must* file a report immediately. If the report covers injury or damage you must file it within five days. Some states may require reports for less serious accidents, so be sure to check out the laws in your state.

If you ever have to file an accident report you must, if the Coast Guard issued your boat numbers, send it to the Coast Guard Officer in Charge of the nearest Marine Inspection Office. Otherwise, you file the report with the state that issued your boat numbers. A special form "Boating Accident Report" form number CG-3865 is available at all Coast Guard Stations and Marine Inspection Offices. (See Appendix 2.) We hope you'll *never* have to fill out one of these forms — just remember, "SAFE BOATING IS NO ACCIDENT".

QUICK QUIZ: (Operation) (answers on page 32)

1. Falls from a slippery floor or deck are always a hazard in boats. Suppose someone fell in your boat, badly spraining his ankle. If he were to be laid up for a week with this injury what is your responsibility with this matter? Jot down your answer here.

   _____

2. Study the sketch below. If you were a Coast Guard Boarding Officer would you send this boat back to the nearest dock? Why?

   _____
   _____
   _____

B. Hazardous Areas

3. Dams

We realize that some Skippers may never operate a boat near a dam, but others will.

Areas that are immediately above and below dams are very dangerous to small boats and you must stay clear. Observe and obey all signs and instructions. At some dams where there is an open spillway, a boat that gets too close could be trapped and swept over the dam. If the dam is part of a hydro-electric power plant there may be areas of extreme water turbulence just below the dam. Very often these power plants operate on a "demand" basis. That is, it might be perfectly calm water just below the dam — then all at once somebody opens a giant valve and there's a raging torrent of water coming out that would capsize any boat. Even people with PFD's on could be dragged under and drowned.

2. Skin Divers

Skin diving is a rapidly growing sport and as you might expect much of it takes place in areas of recreational boating. While operating your boat you must keep a sharp lookout for skin divers. Some dive from a boat while others swim out from shore. Divers will usually display the flag shown in the sketch below:

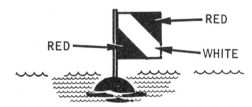

Sometimes this flag is attached to a small floating buoy or an inflated innertube. In all cases stay well clear and watch closely for air bubbles in the water. Slow down and be prepared to stop the engine instantly. Learn to identify and know what to do whenever you spot the diver's flag.

3. Special zoned areas

Just like the divers flag there are other areas zoned and marked that, as the Skipper

of the boat, you should take pains to stay well clear of. For example, study this symbol for a moment:

You may see this symbol on a buoy or on a signboard/flag. Its meaning is simple; it is an area reserved for swimmers — boats STAY OUT! This symbol may also mean DAM, WATERFALL, RAPIDS, etc. and in general means BOATS KEEP OUT!!!

SKINDIVER'S FLAG MEANS BOATS KEEP AWAY

C. Anchoring

Choose the right anchor for your boat and the type of bottom you expect to be anchoring in. Shown below are sketches of some different anchors.

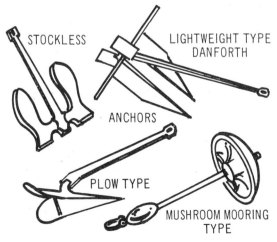

That which is attached to the anchor is called the "rode" (a real salty term). The rode is made of a short piece of chain, various connectors, and the anchor line. Shown below is a sketch of anchoring gear ready for use.

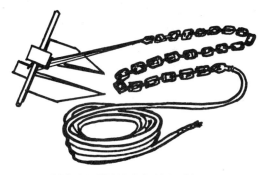

GROUND TACKLE (MADE UP)
DANFORTH ANCHOR SHOWN

Coming up to Anchor

Use some care in selecting the spot to anchor. Boats already anchored own that spot and can't be expected to move so pick a spot that's well clear (even after paying out your anchor line). If available, use buoys as reference points or, if close to shore, use a prominent land feature. Slow down to bare headway, keeping the bow into the wind and/or current, whichever is strongest. As you approach the anchoring point bring the engine to neutral and drift into position. When your boat is dead in the water, let the engine idle in neutral. *Lower*, do not throw, the anchor over the side. Throwing the anchor often causes it to foul with parts of the rode. After the anchor is on the bottom pay out the anchor line gradually as the boat drifts back from the anchor point due to wind or current. As a general rule, pay out three to five times as much anchor line as you have depth of water. If the wind or current is fairly strong, you may have to increase the amount of line you pay out (called the "Scope"). In some cases, (i.e., heavy weather-strong current) you may need a scope of as much as seven times the depth of the water. Take a couple of turns of anchor line around the anchor bit or cleat and tie your favorite hitch — you know — the one that's easy to cast off. Above all keep your feet and legs well clear of the anchor line.

DROPPING ANCHOR

QUICK QUIZ: (Anchoring) (answers on page 34)

1. Complete the following statements:
   An accident report must be filled out and submitted when:
   a. As a result of the accident a _____ is lost.
   b. When anyone is laid-up for ____ hours or more.
   c. Property damage is in excess of _____ dollars.

2. When you see this sign on a buoy it means _____.

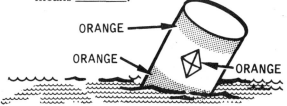

3. When you see this signal on a boat or a float it means: _____.

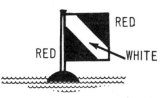

4. When anchoring your boat, never *throw* the anchor because it might _____.

5. After the anchor has a bite (digs in) you will normally pay out anchor line (scope) ____ to ____ times the depth of water.

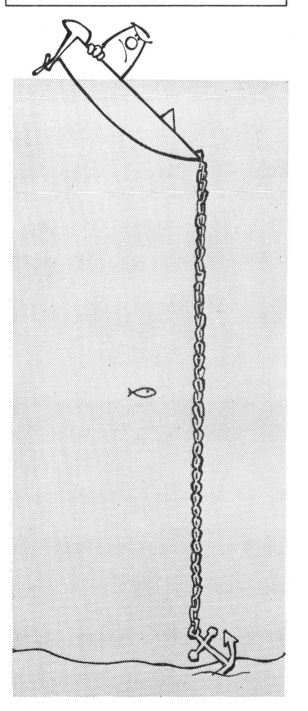

D. Emergency Procedures

1. Man Overboard

The second greatest cause of fatal boating accidents is falling overboard. Many of these accidents happen when the boat is moored. The passengers often haven't had time to adjust to the unstable footing conditions in most small boats. Falling overboard can also be caused by unsafe practices such as sitting on outside decks or gunwales (edges of the boat), or standing or moving about without holding on. There's an old Coast Guard rule that applies here: that is, "one hand for the ship, and one for yourself" meaning "Hang on." Making high-speed, tight turns without warning your passengers, slipping on slippery surfaces or just plain dumb horseplay are other causes.

If someone in your boat falls overboard there are two basic methods you can use to get them back into the boat safely. The first is self-rescue. If somebody falls overboard the first thing to do is get something that floats into the water near the person that he can hang on to. A PFD is *best* but don't delay to hunt for one. An empty gas tank, a styrofoam icebox, an oar, all float and would help keep the victim afloat until you can get something better to him. Stop the boat dead in the water and have the victim swim to the boat. He can see the boat, and with the motor turned off you can talk to him. If the person is hurt or unconscious, or for some reason can't swim to the boat, the second rescue method is used. Again, get something that floats into the water near the victim. Reduce speed and turn back to where the person is. Approach with the bow into the wind or into the current. Shut off the engine completely because even in neutral the propeller can still spin fast enough to injure. When alongside, get a swim ladder over if you have one — if not, help the person back into the boat over the *stern*. If you must go into the water to help — put on a PFD first and hang onto a line.

2. Capsizing

This is the number one killer in boating accidents and the primary cause is overloading or improper loading. It *can* happen for other reasons so you must know what to do. First, *stay with the boat*. Most small boats continue to float even when turned over or full of water. Because of the extra flotation built in,

on wood, mattress, or rags, put it out with water using your bailing bucket (another good reason to carry one), also there's plenty of water around. If the fire is in loose materials it may be best to simply heave them over the side into the water. If the fire is oil, grease, or some kind of fuel you'll have to use your fire extinguisher. Point the nozzle at the base of the flames. A simple fact to remember is that a fire must have fuel, air, and heat. Take away any *one* of the three and it *must* go out.

If you're underway and a fire starts, stop the boat — keep the wind (if any) away from the fire. If the fire is in the back of the boat, head into the wind — if in the bow of the boat, back the stern around to face the wind. Finally, keep your fire extinguisher ready at hand and check pressure gauges each time you go out in the boat.

In case of an explosion, there's not a lot you can do except to get into the water with a PFD. Keep everybody together and get clear of the boat.

the boat will normally float even with the engine still attached to the boat. There's always the temptation to immediately swim ashore. But, when you're in the water you can't correctly judge the distance to shore. It's usually two or three times further than it looks. In addition, you should stay with the boat because it can be more easily seen by other boats and aircraft. Hang onto the boat and if possible, get everyone into a PFD. Once you have done this you must *cooly* evaluate the situation. It is often possible to right a small boat, get back in, and get it closer to shore using oars, paddles, or hands. Finally, be ready to give a distress signal — but save your signals until it's evident that there's a good chance somebody will see it.

QUICK QUIZ: (Emergencies) (answers on page 36)

1. The second greatest cause of fatal boating accidents is:_____.

2. The *first* thing to do when somebody falls overboard from your boat is to: _____.

3. The number one cause of fatal boating accidents is _____ and is due to overloading or improper loading.

4. If your boat ever capsizes, always _____ with the boat.

5. A fire must have three things in order to burn. These are:
   a._____
   b._____
   c._____

3. Fire Afloat

A fire aboard is a very hairy experience — ashore you can usually get away from it — but in a boat you are trapped. When the fire is

4. Lost

Daniel Boone once said that he had never been lost in the forest but he did admit that he had been confused for several days. There *could* be times when you, too, could be confused — or if you want to come right out and say it — "Lost." For example, you might be out fishing some day and all at once a thick fog rolls in and you lose all your bearings. Without these for reference, there's a good chance you'd soon be confused if you tried to go back in to port. In a situation like this don't try to go back in. If you're anchored — stay anchored. If it's too deep to anchor, make up and put out a sea anchor. That is, tie a line to your bailing bucket or an empty portable gas tank. Fill it with water and secure the line to the boat's bow cleat. Use anything that will drag and keep you from drifting. Maintain a sharp lookout all around. Get out your whistles, bell, or horn and make a fog signal — one long toot or ring

every minute. Remember this — you filed a Float Plan, right? OK, we know about where you are — and if you've been reported overdue — we'll come looking for you!! If you have a marine chart of the area you're in, and a boat compass, it's really very difficult to be truly lost. If you do have them and you are lost (for the moment), take the time to study your chart. Then, lay out your compass course to the nearest point you know you'd recognize. The rest should be easy. Look at it this way. On his first voyage to the new world Columbus was lost for many, many days. But he believed in his compass, steered a fixed course, discovered the new world, and *found his way home.*

"GO STRAIGHT AHEAD — YOU CAN'T MISS IT."

1. If you are planning to take your boat into unfamiliar waters you should study a _____ of the area.

2. While not required by law, a useful piece of equipment to use in low visibility is a _____.

3. If anchored in a fog you must make a _____ every _____.

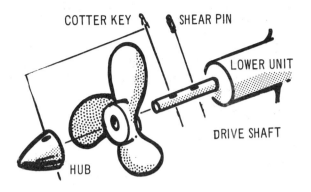

5. Disabled

Usually when a boat is disabled, it is due to some sort of trouble with the engine. For most engines there are three "soft" spots where the trouble is likely to occur. The fuel system, the electrical/ignition system, and the drive train (propeller, shear pin, etc.) cause most of the disabling problems. In the case of outboard engines, drive train trouble usually happens when, in shallow water, the propeller strikes bottom or a rock breaking the shear pin. (The shear pin is supposed to break which prevents serious damage to the engine.) This becomes evident as the engine races with no forward motion of the boat. When this happens shut off the engine and put the ignition key in your pocket. Get out your boat box with spare shear pins and cotter keys and a pair of pliers. Release the reversing locking lever, make sure the engine is in neutral gear, and raise and lock the engine so that the propeller is out of the water.

RAISE OUTBOARD

With the pliers straighten and remove the propeller hub cotter key. It may be necessary to slide the propeller from the drive shaft to remove the broken shear pin. Replace the propeller on the drive shaft and line up the shear pin holes in the propeller and drive shaft. Be careful not to drop the new pin in the water. Insert the new shear pin. Replace the propeller hub on the drive shaft. Replace and bend the new cotter key. Wise skippers carry two spare pins *and* a spare propeller since propeller blades do break off occasionally.

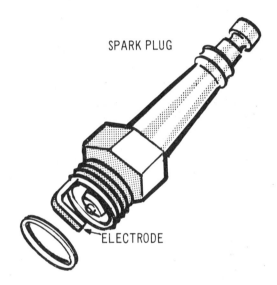

WARNING: Before attempting any electrical repairs, make sure bilges and engine compartments are free of explosive vapors.

When your engine won't start or it quits suddenly, the first and easiest things to check are the spark plugs. Again — to the boat box. Get out the spare plugs and plug wrench (an inexpensive and handy tool). Make sure the engine gears are in neutral and the ignition key (if one is used) is in your pocket. Remove the engine cover. Detach the plug leads and remove the plugs. Inspect the plug electrodes. If they appear oily or black with carbon, replace them with spare plugs. If you don't have a spare plug, try cleaning the electrode.

If plug is OK, check to see that the metal plug gasket is in place and put the plug back in. Look for corroded, dirty, damaged, or loose connections. Check for broken or damaged spark plug wires. Also, check the wiring between the coil and the distributor cap. Dry any wet wiring or connections. If the engine was overheated it may not start until it has cooled.

Fuel problems — check tank. Always check your fuel before leaving the dock. A good rule to follow is never cruise farther than one third of your fuel supply will take you. Save two thirds for the return trip. If there is plenty of gas in the tank, check lines and filter on fuel pump. If no gas is in the bowl the trouble may be a clogged or poorly connected fuel line. Make sure the gas tank vent is open. Remove the sediment bowl and clean the filter, replace the filter and bowl. Disconnect the coil wire from the distributor. Remove the fuel line from the outlet side of the fuel pump and crank the engine. If no fuel comes out of the pump — the pump is the trouble. If fuel is present, reconnect the fuel lines to the carburetor and remove the spark plugs. If they are dry (no fuel on them) the trouble is in the carburetor. Check the choke on the carburetor. Check the adjustment of the main jet.

CAUTION: Don't allow gasoline to spill into the boat.

CARBURETOR

If the plugs are wet the engine may be flooded. Open the throttle wide, put the choke in the full-open position, and with the ignition on, crank over the engine. This draws only air through the engine and will quickly dry it out. For a convenient and more complete booklet on emergency repairs afloat send for a free booklet CG-151 from your nearest Coast Guard district office (see Appendix 2).

QUICK QUIZ: (Repairs) (answers on page 40)

1. Trouble is most likely to occur in a gasoline engine in one of three (3) systems. These systems are:
   a. _____ system
   b. _____ system
   c. _____ system

2. The propeller of an outboard engine is usually protected from damage by a
   _____
   _____

3. A good rule to follow on fuel supply is to use _____ of the fuel for the trip out and reserve the rest for the trip home.

6. Aground

If you boat in tidal waters or in any area where water level is subject to change, there's a chance you might run aground. As in all emergency situations the first thing to do is keep your cool. Usually, your first impulse is to shift immediately into reverse, gun the engine, and attempt to back up. This could be the wrong move. If you were aground on sand or mud the propeller spinning in reverse might pull more sand and mud under the keel making matters worse. Instead, with an oar, paddle, or boat hook test the bottom all around the boat. If the bottom is shallow and sandy and it's safe to do so, get a couple of people out of the boat and push it off. You might get results by having your passengers move and shift their weight. If you've run up on a rock or something solid, check to see if the boat has been holed before you try to back off. It might be wiser to keep the boat on the rock until you're ready to stuff something into the hole. A PFD, mattress, or blanket jammed into the hole may help long enough to get to shore. If the hole is too big, get all hands into a PFD and stay with the boat. It's not going to sink right away if at all.

There's extra flotation in most boats — you and your passengers can hang on until help arrives.

QUICK QUIZ: (Aground) (answers on page 40)

1. If you ever run aground in mud or sand, first check the _____ of the _____.

2. It is often possible to get off from running aground by shifting _____ in the boat.

3. Never get out of the boat to push off without first _____ the bottom.

E. Distress Signals

In general, any signal that will attract attention and bring help is, of course, OK. However, if your signal is a known or recognized distress signal, your chances of getting help are that much better.

First, the visual signals. The most frequently recognized distress signal for small boats on U.S. waters is to slowly and repeatedly *raise and lower your arms, outstretched on each side* as shown in the sketch below.

All other visual signals require some sort of equipment. Although the law does not require you to carry these things they are, for the most part, very inexpensive and can be easily carried in the boat.

A small mirror, and red flares, the same as those used along the road to indicate a car breakdown, can be carried. Flares now come packaged in waterproof containers. Flare pistols and shells also come packaged. Special smoke flares that give off much orange colored smoke are also available — all are easily carried in your boat box. These things are not toys so keep small children away from them and never use them unless you need help.

Many search and rescue craft today carry radar; and there's also a gadget you can carry in your boat called a radar reflector. Most of them are collapsible and store easily. If you're in trouble, you set up the reflector and your boat will show up on the radar screen quite plainly. This helps if we are specifically looking for your boat but will not normally *attract* attention.

Continuously ringing a bell, long blasts on your horn or whistle are also recognized distress signals. At night, or in low visibility, you can use your lights or your flashlight. The international signal on your light for distress is three short flashes, three long flashes, then three short flashes (SOS).

The radiotelephone is probably the best device for calling for help. The Coast Guard stations, ships, and other pleasure craft with radios listen to 2182 kHz. This is the high frequency calling and distress frequency. The very high frequency calling and distress frequency is 156.8 MHz. Radio equipment for this frequency is smaller and likely to be less expensive than that for the lower frequencies. To request life or death emergency assistance on the radiotelephone, use the code words "Mayday, Mayday, Mayday" followed by the emergency message. The Coast Guard has printed a cardboard placard called "Marine Emergency and Distress Information Sheet" (CG-3892) for posting near your radio. You can obtain one from the Coast Guard Auxiliary or the nearest Coast Guard office.

QUICK QUIZ: (Distress) (answers on page 42)

1. A distress message given on radiotelephone is preceded by the words _____.

2. The three letters in International Morse Code used to signify distress are _____ ___.

3. An easily recognized distress signal that does not require equipment is:
    (write your answer in your own words)
    _____
    _____
    _____
    _____

F. Foul Weather Handling

Being caught out in bad weather in a small craft can be a harrowing experience for the new boatman. This is why we say "Keep an eye on the weather." Some types of bad weather cannot be predicted with great accuracy — line squalls, thunderstorms, local fogs and the like. When wind and water start to build, it's time to head for shelter. It is also time to get everybody into a PFD. If there is heavy wave action, you might have to steer the boat so that the bow takes the waves slightly on one side or the other. Be careful to use only enough power to keep your boat heading into the waves — not letting it pound. A little pitching and tossing is a lot safer than rolling. If you have a boat with a high freeboard at the stern it might be safe to turn the stern to the waves and head into shelter. If shelter is not off the bow, and safe to proceed to, then you may have to stay where

you are and *ride out the bad weather.* But that is still up to your judgment. Learn and know your boat's capabilities and limitations in rough water. Outboards with a low transom should never be run in a following sea (where the waves are coming towards the back of the boat) because the waves are often traveling at high speeds and can wash into the boat over the stern — swamping the boat and drowning the engine.

There are certain waters that are best to avoid if at all possible. Examples of these are: river mouths where river currents meet ocean currents or other river currents; areas immediately above and below dams; inlets and harbor entrances where the entrance is narrow and there is shallow water over shoals. In all of these there can be treacherous cross-currents and heavy, choppy water. These can get the unwary Skipper into trouble. A fundamental rule for all Skippers when it comes to "White Water" might well be — don't take chances.

QUICK QUIZ: (Foul weather) (answers on page 42)

1. The first thing to do if ever caught out in bad weather in your boat is to: _____
    _____

2. When heading into heavy waves it is generally best to steer the boat so that the waves hit the boat: _____
    _____

3. Running before a following sea (where the waves are coming towards the back of the boat) is dangerous when the boat has a low _____ at the stern.

G. Review

In PART III you learned what is considered negligent operation. Keep in mind that at no time does the Coast Guard want to spoil anyone's boating fun — we want you to live it up — but live!!!

Hazardous areas were next and examples were described so that you can avoid them in the future. When operating your boat, remember to avoid areas immediately above and below dams, wherever you see the skin diver's flag, and areas marked for swimming. Anchoring was the next subject and you learned about making up "ground tackle" and the right way to set it out. By far one of the most important sections was next — emergency procedures. The steps to be carried out for man overboard, capsizing, fire aboard, lost, disabled, or aground. We want to remind you again to be sure you know what to do and how to do it for each of these emergency situations. The best way is to practice with drills. We do it and we're professional — why not try it out. Finally, a short section on handling your boat in fog and rough water. It is not possible to cover all situations in this program and much remains for you to learn through experience.

By far the best way for you to learn *all* the things you should know about boating is to take one of the formal safe boating courses from either the Coast Guard Auxiliary or the U.S. Power Squadrons. These courses are given by experienced boatmen who can give you many valuable tips about operating your boat.

Review Exercise, Part III Underway

The following problems are of the situational type where you are asked to apply what you have learned to solve a problem. In most cases, you will find, if you look closely small clues that might help in determining the right answer. (Answers page 44)

1. Having seen all the fun that Charlie and Zelda were having, Charlie Noble's friend Irving Plimsole bought a boat, motor, and trailer. Charlie was trying very hard to teach Irving the principles of boating safety, but from time to time found it a trying experience. Take the time that Charlie and Irving decided to take both boats and families to the lake for a joint cruise. All went well until Irving started to back away from the fuel pier. With the engine in reverse Irving opened the throttle wide intending to show Charlie what a sharp boat operator he was. The stern swung around too fast and slammed into Charlie's engine cover, damaging it more than merely somewhat. "Oops!" said Irving, "don't worry Charlie, my insurance will pay for a new cover." "That's all very well," Charlie said, (gritting his teeth) "but that cover will cost over $150 and there's something else you'll have to do."

What do you think Charlie has in mind?" Jot down your answers and go on to the next question.

_____
_____
_____
_____
_____
_____
_____

2. Charlie and Irving planned to cruise up to the head of the lake and anchor at a spot where the fishing was good and the swimming was great. However, having been there before, Charlie wanted to make sure that Irving would be aware that there were areas to be avoided. "Irving," Charlie said, "A lot of people like to skin dive where we're going and the swimming area itself is forbidden to boats, so if you see either of these signs — stay well clear." Charlie quickly drew sketches of the two signs Irving was to stay away from.

Draw simple sketches of the signs Irving is to avoid then go on to the next problem.

3. After an uneventful but enjoyable cruise up the lake, Charlie and Irving arrived at the quiet little cove where they planned to anchor for the day. 'I'll go in and anchor first then you anchor up ahead of me," Charlie shouted to Irving. Charlie then got out his ground tackle (anchor, chain and line) from the bow cuddy. He carefully made up the anchor line in coils and placed it on the bow. Using small amounts of power he drifted up to the spot where he wanted the anchor to dig in. When the boat was dead in the water he lowered the anchor to the bottom in 20 feet of water. Noting that there was little breeze and no current, Charlie put the engine in slow reverse and paid out the anchor line to the proper scope.

How much line do you think Charlie used for the proper scope? Write your answer then go to the next question.

_____

_____

_____

_____

4. *With his boat securely anchored and the engine shut off, Charlie signaled to Irving to come up to anchor. Irving turned the controls over to his wife Porta and climbed up in the bow to get his anchor ready. Porta steered toward the stern of Charlie's boat where Irving intended to anchor. All at once she realized she was coming too fast so she put the engine in reverse and gave it the gas. The* boat *stopped as if it hit a brick wall — but Irving didn't — he kept on going — right over the bow and into the water. Charlie, realizing that Irving wasn't an Olympic swimmer, immediately did the right thing.*

What would you do in Charlie's place?

_____

_____

_____

_____

_____

5. *Most of the rest of the day was uneventful with Irving giving serious thought to taking a boating safety course from the Coast Guard Auxiliary as Charlie had done. However, along about early afternoon, heavy black clouds were observed down the lake in the direction of the marina and heading right for them. Heavy rain and gusts of wind could be seen whipping the water into white caps. Irving and Porta wanted to head back to the marina and launching ramp. Charlie recognized that the storm was a thunder squall that although very dangerous would quickly blow over.*

What do you think he did? Write down your answer.

_____

_____

_____

_____

PART IV, RETURNING TO PORT

A. Mooring (Docking)

On the open water, a boat seems to respond like a car. It even has the "feel" of a car. Problem is, though, it isn't a car. It doesn't have brakes, for one thing. And it gets its steering orders from the rear, not the front. The "road" it's on isn't solid like concrete, but is moving and changing with wind, tide, and current.

But, because a boat feels like a car on open water, our reflexes take over, and at first we drive a boat as we would a car. This can be extremely hazardous. The wake of the boat can upset other craft, the swinging stern can produce a surprise collision with moored objects such as buoys or other boats. Since the roadway is "alive" with tide, wind, and current, but our reflexes are treating it as a solid mass, we can quickly find ourselves totally out of control.

The waters near a dock should *always* be treated with the same respect and caution as a road you suspect might be slippery — where a sudden turn or change of speed could leave you out of control.

Every time you approach a docking area, you should use the same intelligence you'd use in testing a road for your car. Slow down. Try the rudder, speed up a bit — get the feel of the road and the response of the boat. *Re-educate* your senses and reflexes. Watch the stern when you make a turn. *See* where it swings. Now, and only now, are you ready to approach the dock. (This is a good time, too, to put out your fenders.)

Approach the dock slowly, with alternating stop/slow-advance/stop/advance actions. The water will be different a second from now — don't presume you have mastered it. If possible, approach the dock into the wind and current — unless, of course, you just intend to wave to friends in passing. Wind and current may not be in the same direction. Select the stronger force, and drive against it. This way, you have power and control.

BACK UP AND COME IN SLOWER.

Thirty degrees is a good approach angle. It's about the angle you'd use to approach a curb with your car if you were parallel parking.

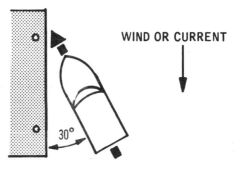

WIND OR CURRENT

30°

As the bow nears the dock, swing slowly parallel to it. (Think of the boat as a car with nice, clean, whitewalls you've just spent half a day cleaning!) Tie up the bow line first. (If you tied up stern line first, the bow could be blown or carried by current into the open water near the dock, creating a hazard for other boats and possibly causing extensive damage to your own.)

1. Since the property damage to Charlie's boat was in excess of $100, Irving must fill out and submit an accident report.

2.

3. Under these conditions three to five times the depth of the water would be OK or 60 to 100 feet of line.

4. Charlie snatched up a PFD and threw it into the water *near* where Irving was paddling in angry circles.

5. Both boats were in a protected cove so Charlie persuaded Irving to stay put. He then increased the scope of his anchor line to seven times the depth and they safely rode out the brief storm.

have to put the motor in slow reverse as you approach the dock. Approach at a slight angle this time and gently swing parallel; but HAVE THE *STERN* line ready: — and tie *it* on first this time!

Docking is really something that takes practice, much as it took practice (and no substitute for it) to learn how to back a car into a parallel parking spot.

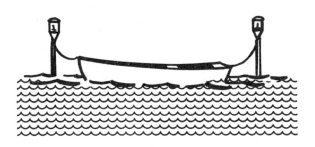

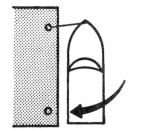

Tie up bow and stern. If you are in a tidal area, the lines should be at about a 45-degree angle to the boat — that'll leave enough line for the boat to safely rise or fall with the tide.

If, as you approach the mooring, the wind and/or current are moving toward the dock make your move parallel to the dock a bit further out and let the wind/current push you over the dock.

Occasionally, you're going to have to approach a dock with the wind or current on your stern, or behind you. This is a difficult and sometimes dangerous maneuver. Depending on the speed of wind or current, you may

QUICK QUIZ: (Docking) (answers on page 46)

1. Approaching a dock, it is wise to stop the boat, then slowly advance, and alternate between the two, in order to _____ our senses.

2. Approaching a dock, if possible, have the wind, tide or current (whichever is the stronger) Ahead/Behind you (select right one).

3. The basic rule for docking is like that for a car; always operate your vehicle so that you are in control. To stay in control through docking, attach the _____ line first, when you've approached the dock against the wind/current, and the _____ line first when you've approached it with the wind or current to your back.

4. Safe boating is a matter of common sense and courtesy, based on some simple, proven rules. No course on boat-

ing can answer all the problems that may occur, but it can and should provide a "sense" of conduct that can be projected to other situations. What if you were coming into a dock and made your approach letter perfect, only to find someone else was either docking or leaving, totally ignoring your approach. Of course, he shouldn't, but there you are — and it'll happen. What do you think you should do, as a safe boater?

B. Securing Equipment

There are two "secure" positions for equipment, and these are the only positions they should ever be stowed in. One is storage, the other "standby" or "ready." Before you get underway, all equipment should be in a ready position — PFD's out of storage and available — horn uncovered — working lines coiled and available — fire extinguishers handy.

As much as good docking is a matter of habit, it is equally as good a habit to secure all equipment before going ashore. That is the *only* way you'll know where it is the next time you go out.

We have provided you with a list of required and some recommended equipment. It represents the minimum necessary for safe boating. But, "Proof of Purchase" is not a reasonable facsimile for equipment lost or stolen. Make a place for it. A secure place.

The biggest and most expensive piece of "equipment" you have is your boat. To secure it, you need good lines, but the best line is only as good as your worst knot.

QUICK QUIZ: (Equipment) (answers on page 46)

1. There are two "secure positions" for equipment _____ and _____.

2. Your boat is/isn't a piece of equipment.

3. The Coast Guard list of required equipment is the maximum/minimum required for safe boating.

C. Returning the Boat to the Trailer

OK, you've returned to port. The boat is moored or docked near the ramp. Now you're going ashore to get the car and trailer. So, may as well take as much along with you as you can, right?

Wrong.

Don't try to carry bulky loads on or off the boat. That's a great way to have an accident. Remember, the roadway under the boat is alive and moving! Stow equipment that you are bringing ashore on the dock, piece by piece. Then, when ashore, you can carry a full load of gear on the ground, which doesn't move much.

Back the trailer to the ramp. As with unloading, only one person in the car and one person directing as you back the trailer to the water's edge. Parking gear isn't safe enough. Set the handbrake, too.

Before loading the boat onto the trailer, be certain the motor is in the tilted or upward position and securely locked.

Pull the boat onto the trailer with a bow line. When it's properly aligned, you can winch it aboard. Secure the tie-downs and

45

check the hitch on the car. If the motor is clamped to a transom, check the clamps before starting out — they could have loosened from vibration while on the water.

When pulling out from the ramp, remember the trailer wheels aren't on the rear of the trailer — when the trailer turns, the overhang will swing. Have someone guide you away from the ramp, at least until the trailer is clear and aligned behind you.

QUICK QUIZ: (Trailering) (answers on page 48)

1.   When returning the boat to the trailer, there should be _____ person(s) in the boat.

2.   How many people should be in the car when backing the trailer to the ramp? How many giving driver directions _____.

3.   At what speed should the boat be driven on the trailer? _____.

4.   What is the proper position of the motor drive unit when reloading the boat? _____.

D. Cancel Float Plan

In previous lessons you learned the reasons for filing a Float Plan with a relative or neighbor. You also learned the very good reasons for cancelling the Float Plan when you return. Make both of these a boating habit. You can help conserve the Coast Guard's search and rescue resources for when they are truly needed. A wild goose chase could be very expensive when someone forgets to cancel his Float Plan. So, with the boat all snug in its slip, mooring, or back on the trailer at home — cancel the Float Plan!

E. Review

A smart Skipper realizes that operating a boat requires a different set of reflexes than those required for operating a car. These reflexes can only be acquired by practice. At first, operating a boat might seem like driving a car. But the wise Skipper remembers the boat does not have brakes and learns to maneuver his boat accordingly.

Mooring or docking a boat bears small likeness to parking a car. Wind and current and their direction and force dictate how the maneuver is to be accomplished. Safe Skippers are smart enough to realize they'll never quite "know it all." As a result they continue to practice and learn. This is how they live long enough to acquire the title "Ancient Mariner."

Safe boating is a series of good habits based for the most part on common good sense. Acquire and maintain the habit of always putting your equipment where it belongs, either in storage when not on the water, or in standby when underway.

For those Skippers who trailer their boat, loading or unloading a boat from a trailer is serious business. There may be thousands of pounds of force at work. The danger lies in carelessness. Most of the time all goes well — until the one time it doesn't — then it's too late. Launch and load the boat with your trailer the safe way. No short cuts — by the numbers every time.

Finally, all boating trips that have a happy ending — end with the Skipper cancelling his Float Plan.

3. In the sketch below Charlie and Zelda are unloading the boat before loading the boat back on the trailer. (Which is a good idea.)

However, if you look close you might see that Charlie is not as safe as he could be. What is he doing wrong?

_____
_____
_____

Review Exercise Part IV (Returning to Port) (answers on page 50)

1. Charlie and Zelda Noble were returning to dock and launching area after a perfect day of fishing and swimming. As they approached the dock, Charlie, instead of giving the maneuvers his full attention, was mentally adding to the length and weight of the fish he had caught. All at once Charlie woke up to the fact that he was nearing the dock at far too great a speed. In order to avoid crashing into the dock Charlie had to put the engine in full reverse which barely stopped the boat in time.

What *should* Charlie have done as he neared the dock first? Write down your answer before going on.

_____
_____
_____
_____

2. Zelda, as befits a good Skipper's Mate, had gotten Charlie's new fenders out and rigged them properly over the side of the boat. She then got the mooring lines and made them up in loose coils ready to use. One for the bow mooring cleat and another for the stern. "Charlie," Zelda asked, "which line should I use first?" Charlie, noting the wind was blowing over the stern of the boat, pointed to one of the lines and said "that one."

Which line do you think Charlie pointed to?

_____
_____

4. Zelda went to the parking lot, got the car and trailer and slowly backed down to the water. She had become quite skillful at this through much practice, instruction, and several spirited discussions with Charlie. She carefully set the handbrake and parking gear and turned off the engine. She got out of the car and unreeled several feet of winch line. Charlie then eased the bow of the boat onto the back of the trailer, lined up the center line and gave the engine the gun. Zelda then snapped the winch line hook to the bow.

Do you think they did anything wrong? If so, what?

_____
_____
_____
_____
_____
_____

5. With the boat back on the trailer, Charlie drove off well clear of the ramp area and parked. While Zelda was loading the car Charlie climbed into the boat to open the drain plug, check the engine clamps for tightness, and checked all his safety gear for proper stowage. He then installed his hold-down clamps and drew them up tight. It being nearly dusk, Charlie and Zelda operated all the car and trailer lights and found them to be OK. Giving the trailer safety chains one last check, Charlie then drove home. While Zelda unloaded the car, Charlie got out his garden hose and rinsed the boat thinking all the while of the fun he and Zelda had that day.

Do you think Charlie is through yet? Isn't there one more thing he should do?

_____

_____

_____

_____

_____

PART V, AIDS TO SAFE BOATING

A. Introduction

In this, the final part of this program we have a special problem. This problem simply stated is: there is no way we can know where you, the reader of this program, will be operating your boat. Water areas for recreational boating in the United States include Rivers, Great Lakes, and of course the thousands of lakes and streams. These water areas have different requirements for Rules of the Road, required lights for boats, and even buoy marking systems. As you can see we are faced with two alternatives. First, we could ask you to learn *all* the area rules, lights and buoy systems. But then you would learn a number of things you might have little or no use for. Instead, in the following lessons you will learn the rules that apply to a majority of boatmen. In turn, many of these rules can be applied with easily learned differences to the rules for other areas. There are several detailed treatments available on rules of the road for your area. These include: Rules of the Road for International and Inland Waters are combined in CG-169. For the Great Lakes it's CG-172 and for the Western Rivers CG-184. To obtain any one of these booklets, refer to Appendix 2 for the address of the Coast Guard Office nearest you. Appendix 4 lists many other useful boating texts.

The Western Rivers Rules of the Road apply to specific inland waters of the United States. They are not applicable to rivers on the West Coast, such as the Sacramento and Columbia, that empty into the Pacific Ocean.

Obviously the Great Lakes rules refer to the Great Lakes and some of the principal river regions close to them. The term "Western Rivers" DOES NOT refer to rivers of the western United States, but instead to the Mississippi River and associated rivers. The general area is shown in the map below. Anyone boating in that area — or in any other area — should check to see which rules apply for them.

The Inland Rules apply to all U.S. waters not covered by Great Lakes or Western Rivers rules. Generally, the International rules apply to waters on the high seas — but like all generalizations, there are exceptions.

While having rules with so many exceptions can be frustrating, it is equally true that the differences represent just plain good sense where they exist. WHEREVER you are boating, you should find out which rules apply to you and your boat.

QUICK QUIZ: (Rules) (answers on page 50)

1. There are four different sets of Rules of the Road. These are detailed in three (3) Coast Guard Booklets:
    (fill in the blanks)
    a. CG-169 _____ and _____
    b. CG-172 _____
    c. CG-184 _____

2. The rules of the road used on the Mississippi River are the _____

3. Generally, in all other water areas not covered by Western Rivers or Great Lakes rules the _____ rules will apply.

B. Rules of the Road

In this lesson the situations, signals, and actions taken are based on the INLAND RULES of the Road which most Skippers will use. First, some terms and definitions.

There is much similarity between the marine "Rules of the Road" and the rules we use in driving a car. And just like automotive rules, they exist to help everyone avoid collisions and accidents.

In discussing rules of the road, we're going to use two special terms: "Privileged" and "Burdened" boats. The privileged boat is the one with the *right of way*. The burdened

ANSWERS: (Exercise) (page 47)

1. Charlie should have stopped dead in the water, well clear of the dock for a moment, paid full attention to wind and water conditions, — then eased into the dock with short spurts of power.
2. With the wind blowing from the stern, Charlie pointed to the stern line.
3. He should keep *both* feet in the boat and hand the gear up to the dock.
4. Charlie shouldn't have driven the boat onto the trailer — it should be winched on. Remember — the boat hasn't any brakes and Charlie could have ended up with several feet of bow sticking through the rear window.
5. No — not quite. He must now cancel his Float Plan.

ANSWERS: (Rules) (page 49)

1. a. Inland International
   b. Great Lakes
2. c. Western Rivers
3. Inland-International

vessel is the one with the *"burden of responsibility"* for taking whatever action is best to avoid a collision.

On shore, in an automobile, when we wish to pass or turn, we provide either a hand signal, signal with a directional light, or give a toot on the horn. The purpose is to make certain the other drivers know what you are going to do — so that they won't take some other action that might cause an accident. We do the same things on the water, but use either a whistle or horn.

The length of the blasts, or toots is part of the signalling code. A Prolonged Blast is one of 4 to 6 seconds long.

A Long Blast is 8 to 10 seconds.

A Short Blast is of about one-second duration.

We all know it does no good to have 20 car horns blowing in a traffic jam. So too, with the rules afloat. Use your whistle signals *only* when the situation requires them.

Further, when there is clearly no danger of collision, no signals are required — anymore than on shore with a car.

Again, rules of the road are just common sense. Action should be taken when it is *clear* that a potentially dangerous situation exists. The action should be CLEAR and DECISIVE

and be taken early enough to be noticed and understood by the other boat.

Again, common sense — large vessels can't stop quickly, change course or generally maneuver as well as a small boat. Also, large vessels in harbors and rivers must stay with the channels. They have the right of way and the burden to avoid collisions is on the Skipper of the smaller boat.

The danger signal where Inland Rules apply is four short blasts or toots. When you hear it, you must slow down and maneuver as necessary or stop until the danger condition — or confusion — has been resolved.

Sailboats, under sail, lack the means of control that may be required for decisive and timely action. Therefore, they have the right of way over a powered boat (but not over large vessels in confined or narrow channels).

There are three types of situations between two approaching vessels that require whistle signals to be given. These are: Meeting, crossing, and overtaking.

Meeting head-on or nearly so: just as in driving a car, you stay more to your right. One boat gives a single short blast; the other responds with the same signal. Now each Skipper knows what the other is going to do — and they've confirmed it.

What about meeting but passing well clear of each other — the only time boats may pass each other to the right (starboard-to-starboard)? Again, just common sense — to suddenly change course in order to pass the other boats left side would create a dangerous situation. Don't count on the other Skipper to know that; instead, give him two short blasts. He'll answer with two, and you'll both be relieved that you communicate so well.

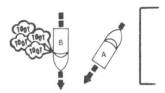

If, at any time, there is confusion about signals or intent, four short blasts is the danger signal — each boat must come to stop until the situation is clarified. This occurs when one boat gives a proper passing signal, and the other confirms it. In this situation boat A is backing away from a dock and may not see boat B who then sounds the danger signal.

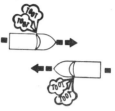

A crossing situation is similar to meeting another car at an intersection that has no stop signs. As ashore, the vehicle to the right is privileged — in fact, he *must* continue his course and speed. Inland rules do not require signals in this situation, but again, common sense should prevail. The boat on the right (privileged) should signal his intent to maintain his course and speed by one short horn blast. The burdened vessel should reply with a short blast signalling his intent to slow down and/or change course to pass astern of the other boat.

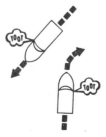

Finally, there are the overtaking situations. Normally, you'd pass the privileged vessel on his left, as you would in a car, and signal this intent with two short blasts. If it is safe to pass, the privileged vessel will respond with two short blasts. Then the burdened boat passes keeping well clear of the privileged boat.

If it is more reasonable to pass on the privileged boat's right, signal your intent with one short blast. A one short blast reply gives the go ahead.

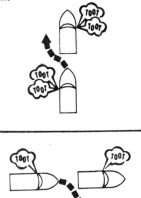

Should the privileged vessel consider it unsafe for you to pass as you proposed, it must reply with four short blasts (the danger signal). The burdened vessel must then remain in position and make no further attempt to pass until the privileged vessel answers a one or two short blast signal with one or two short blasts respectively, or proposes a new signal.

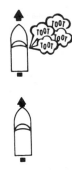

When a boat is ready to leave a dock, slip, or mooring — normally the boat is backed out into the regular traffic channel. Few boats maneuver well when going astern and you will be entering an area where there may be several other boats underway. The rules of the road require that you sound one long blast on the horn or whistle (8 to 10 seconds) as soon as you clear the dock or slip.

This signal must also be sounded when approaching a blind bend in a river or channel. This signal would warn any boat approaching the bend from the other direction. Once in sight of each other, normal rules of the road and maneuvering signals apply.

QUICK QUIZ: (Signals) (answers on page 54)

A sample of meeting, crossing, and overtaking problems are shown in the little sketches below. Inland rules apply to these situations.

1. Boats A and B are on courses that will allow them to pass well clear without maneuvering. What sound signals do they each give?

Boat A sounds_____ short blast(s). Boat B replies with____. short blast(s). (note: a blast is the same as a TOOT!)

2. Here boats A and B are meeting head on. What signals do they exchange and what course changes do they make?

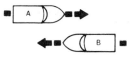

Boat A sounds_____ blast(s). Boat B replies with_____blast(s).

3. In this situation one boat is said to be ___ and the other is _____
   a. Boat A is _____
   b. Boat B is _____

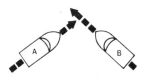

c. What must boat A do (in your own words)? _____

d. What must boat B do? _____

e. *If he wishes* boat B may give _____ short blast(s). _____

4. In this case boat A is overtaking boat B and wishes to pass boat B on B's *right*.

a. Boat A is the _____ boat.

b. Boat B is the _____ boat.

c. Boat A sounds _____ short blast(s).

d. Boat B replies with ___ short blast(s).

5. Shown below is another overtaking situation. Boat A wishes to pass boat B on B's left side. However, Boat B sees a potentially dangerous condition ahead that Boat A may not be able to see (another boat anchored ahead.)

a. Boat A sounds _____ short blast(s).

b. Boat B sounds _____ short blast(s).

c. What does boat A do now?
   (in your own words)

_____
_____
_____
_____

C. Navigation Lights

Federal law requires that ALL boats display certain lights at night. These lights will tell others of your presence, what kind of a boat you are: that is, sailboat, motorboat, and even a rowboat. These lights on another boat will tell you whether you're meeting, crossing, or overtaking another boat.

Only three (3) colors are used: red, green, and white. A red light is displayed on the bow's *left* or port side. An easy way to remember is *"Port wine is Red."* A green light is displayed on the bow and indicates the right or *starboard* side. White lights are usually displayed on the back (stern) of boats but may be found on other parts of the boat, especially on larger vessels.

In addition to the colors used and the position of the lights on a boat, lights are "shaded" so that they cannot be seen from certain directions. The amount of light that can be seen from a shaded light is measured in "Points." A point is equal to eleven and one quarter degrees ($11\frac{1}{4}°$) of a circle. For example an unshaded light that can be seen from *any* direction would be called a 32 point light because:

$$32 \times 11.25° = 360°$$

A 10 point light can be seen through an arc of $112\frac{1}{2}$ degrees. Shown below are examples of 10 point lights as viewed looking down on the top of the lights. Ten point lights are always red or green.

10-POINT (TOP VIEW)

Some of these lights must be bright enough to be seen at least a mile and others must be bright enough to be seen for two (2) miles.

These are twelve (12) and twenty (20) point lights:

12-POINT   20-POINT

and this is a thirty-two (32) point light which of course means it is un-shaded and can be seen from any direction. Twelve, twenty, and thirty-two point lights are always white.

32-POINT

QUICK QUIZ: (Lights) (answers on page 56)

1. Navigation lights installed on a boat tell you:
   a. The class of a boat.
   b. How fast a boat is going.
   c. Whether you are meeting, crossing, or overtaking another boat.
   d. All of the above.
2. The only colors used for navigation lights are:
   a. _____
   b. _____
   c. _____ (In any order)

3. The amount of visibility in shaded lights used for navigation on boats is measured in _____.

4. Only four different "points" of visibility are used for navigation lights. There are:
   a. _____
   b. _____
   c. _____
   d. _____

5. A "point" equals____degrees of visibility.

I'LL DRINK TO THAT!

AN EASY WAY TO REMEMBER IS: "PORT WINE IS RED".

5. The following describes the lights that boats must have installed if not equipped for international use. These requirements apply to boats operated on inland waters, western rivers, and Great Lakes.

First, motorboats that are under twenty-six (26) feet:

a. a combination red and green 20 pt. light displayed on the bow bright enough to be seen *one* mile.

b. a white 32 pt. light displayed on the stern bright enough to be seen two miles. The sketch below summarizes the placement of these lights.

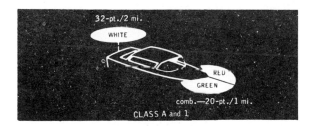

Motorboats of 26 feet to 65 feet (Class 2 and 3) have one more light added. Both the placement and number of points are somewhat different also. The sketch below displays the placement, number of points, colors, and required visibility distances. Study the sketch for a moment and note the differences between light requirements for Class A and 1 motorboats and Class 2 and 3.

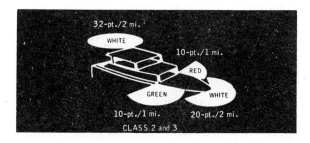

Boats that have both sails and engines, often called auxiliaries, have the same requirements as motorboats. Compare the sketches below with the motorboat sketches.

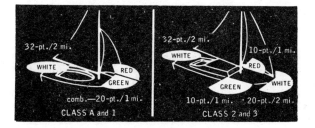

When an auxiliary sailboat is operated at night under sail *alone*, the required lights are slightly different. Under sail *alone* the stern light must be a 12 point light. Of course, with these lights the engine cannot be used at night. Compare the sketches below with the previous sketches and note the differences.

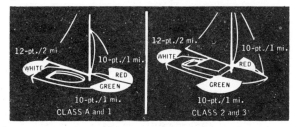

Sailboats with no engine of any kind and sailing at night might display the lights shown in the sketch below.

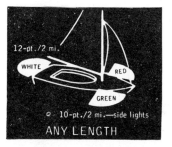

Rowboats and canoes must have ready at hand a lantern showing a white light which is to be temporarily exhibited in sufficient time to prevent collision.

In summary then, when you learn and remember the lights required, you will be able to:

be sure that *your* boat has proper lights;

distinguish between a motorboat, or sailboat;

determine if you are in a meeting, crossing or overtaking situation, and you can get a good idea of how big the other boat is.

The lights required for boats which plan to operate at night on the ocean and outside of inland water must conform to those required by the International Rules of the Road (see chart below). It may be best to have "International" navigation lights in-

ANSWERS: (Lights) (page 54)

1. c.
2. red, green, white
3. points
4. 10, 12, 20, 32
5. 11¼

stalled on your boat since the lights required by the International Rules may also be displayed on inland waters in place of those lights required by Inland Rules.

The most significant difference in International Rules is that the 10 point colored lights (red and green) may be displayed *either* as a combination light or a *separate* side light on all vessels under 65 feet in length. The 32-point white lights are not used, instead a 20-point white light is displayed on the forward part of the vessel and a 12 point white light is shown from the stern.

QUICK QUIZ: (Lights/Inland) (answers on page 58)

Try to answer these questions without referring to the sketches. Inland rules apply.
1. You are following *directly* behind another boat at night heading back to port. What color and what lights would you expect to see? Jot down your answer and go on to the question. _____

2. You and another motorboat are meeting directly head to head. The other boat is 26 feet in length. What color and what lights would you expect to see? Remember, *you* are looking at him. _____

3. While proceeding out for some late night fishing you observe these lights off your *port* bow as shown:

WHITE ●
GREEN ✷ ● WHITE

a. Are you in a meeting, crossing or overtaking situation?
b. Is the other boat under 26 feet in length or over 26 feet?

c. Are you the burdened or privileged boat? _____
_____
_____

4. While proceeding at night in your boat you observe the lights shown below off your starboard bow:

RED ✷ ● WHITE

a. Meeting, crossing, or overtaking?
b. Is the other boat under or over 26 feet in length?
c. Is he the burdened or privileged boat?

D. Aids to Navigation

1. Introduction

In this, the final lesson, we have the same sort of problem that we had for Rules of the Road and required lights for boats. There are several buoy marking systems. What buoys you will see and what they mean will often depend on where you operate your boat. As before, there is no way we can know where you, the reader, will be operating your boat. In this lesson we will concentrate on the two buoy systems that are most common. These are the LATERAL (on which other systems are based) and the UNIFORM STATE WATERWAY MARKING system. If you wish details on the INTRACOASTAL WATERWAY SYSTEM send for CG-193 (See Appendix 2 for address).

Aids to Navigation take the place on the water of street signs and road maps used on land. Aids to navigation are placed at various points along the coasts, rivers, lakes, channels, harbors, etc., as markers and guides to help you locate your position with respect to the shore and to hidden dangers.

All aids to navigation are protected by law. It is not only a VIOLATION OF COMMON SENSE, BUT A CRIMINAL OFFENSE, to cause any damage or hindrance to the proper operation of any aid. Do NOT deface, alter, move or destroy any aid to

required on high seas, may be used inland. 10-point colored lights may be displayed as a combination light or separate side lights on all vessels less than 65 feet in length.

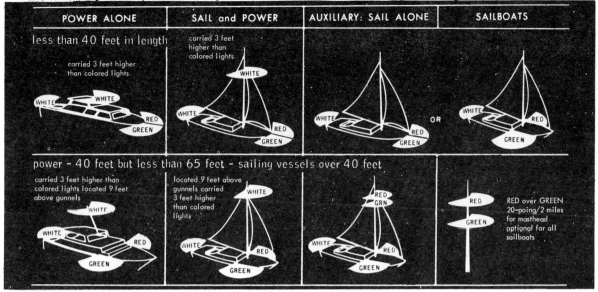

POWER ALONE	SAIL and POWER	AUXILIARY: SAIL ALONE	SAILBOATS
less than 40 feet in length carried 3 feet higher than colored lights	carried 3 feet higher than colored lights		
power - 40 feet but less than 65 feet - sailing vessels over 40 feet			
carried 3 feet higher than colored lights located 9 feet above gunnels	located 9 feet above gunnels carried 3 feet higher than colored lights		RED over GREEN 20-poing/2 miles for masthead optional for all sailboats

navigation. Never tie your boat to a buoy, daybeacon or light structure. AVOID anchoring so close to a buoy that you obstruct the aid from the sight of another boat. If you should unintentionally or unavoidably COLLIDE with or DAMAGE an aid to navigation, this must be reported to the proper authorities.

There are differences in traffic laws between states; there are also differences in systems for operating on different bodies of water. The next few pages will talk about

FISHING FOR TROUBLE.

these different systems known as the LATERAL and UNIFORM STATE buoy systems.

A detailed booklet "Aids to Marine Navigation in the United States" (CG-193) is available. This booklet covers *all* the systems in full detail. You may send for this publication by finding the Coast Guard office nearest you in Appendix 2 of this program.

QUICK QUIZ: (Aids) (answers on page 58)

1. Water borne street signs (buoys, daybeacons, ranges, daymarks, lights, etc.) are the same all over the United States.
   ☐ a. True
   ☐ b. False
2. The term "aid to navigation" as used in this program includes:
   ☐ a. Conspicuous shapes and objects on shore, such as mountain tops, smoke stacks, radio antenna, etc.
   ☐ b. Objects that have been primarily placed in location to assist in navigation.
   ☐ c. Charts, instruments, devices, methods, etc.
3. Our different buoy systems are based on the_____ system.
4. All "aids to navigation" are protected by
_____
5. Information on all of the buoy systems can be found in Coast Guard booklet CG-_____.

NAVIGATIONAL AIDS (BUOYS)

2. The Lateral System

You can find your way around on the water using buoys and the appropriate charts. The *shape* of a buoy, its *color*, the *number* painted on it, and, when it is lighted, the *light* characteristics all will tell you what to do when piloting your boat.

This buoy is called a CAN buoy because of its cylinder-like shape.

Most of the buoys with this shape will be painted BLACK. The number is always odd, that is 3, 5, 7, 9, and so on. You might see a black can buoy that looks like this:

This type of buoy is normally found marking the left side of a channel (as you returned from seaward) and often are used to mark obstructions.

The unusual arrangement on the top of this buoy is called a "Radar Reflector" which causes it to stand out better on a radar screen. The meaning of this buoy is the same as that of a regular black can buoy.

From time to time you may see a can buoy painted in red and black stripes like this:

It won't have a number on it, however. This buoy will mark the junction of two channels.

This buoy is called a NUN buoy, again because of its shape. Most of these buoys will be painted solid red and have *white* even numbers on them — 2, 4, 6, etc. Nun buoys are almost always used to mark the right side of a channel, as you return from seaward.

Other NUN buoys may be painted with horizontal red and black stripes. Like striped can buoys, these buoys also mark channel junctions. Like this:

The buoy shown here is a LIGHTED buoy. It may have any of the aforementioned colorings, which define its meaning. It has a light (and sometimes a radar reflector, bell, gong, or whistle) so it may be more easily located in times of low visibility.

Finally, this buoy is called a SPAR buoy, and may be red with even numbers or black with odd numbers. These buoys usually mark the edge of a channel and are sometimes found marking obstructions. The spar buoy is not very common.

CAN BUOY

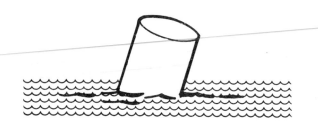

1. a. This buoy is called a _____ buoy.
    b. Most of the time its color will be_____.
    c. If a number is on it, it will be (odd-even). (choose one)_____.

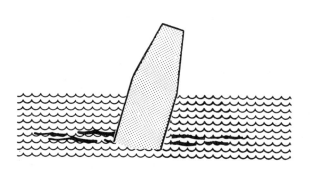

2. a. This buoy is called a_____ buoy.
    b. Most of the time its color will be_____.
    c. If a number is on it, it will be (odd-even). (choose one)_____.

3. a. This buoy is called a_____ buoy.
    b. The color(s) will be_____.
    c. The numbers will be_____.

4. a. This buoy is called a_____ buoy.
    b. The color(s) will be_____.
    c. The numbers will be_____.

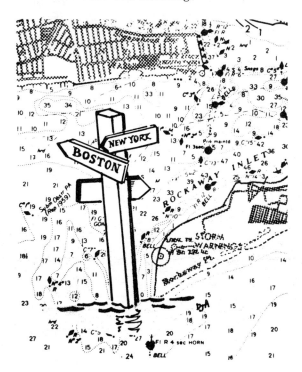

5. In periods of low visibility *some* buoys can be located by their lights or_____.

Summary

As you've learned, buoys are, in effect, floating signposts for the boatmen. By their color, shape, number, light, or sound characteristics, they tell you how to avoid hazards and aid you in following a safe course. It is best to compare a chart of the area with these aids to see their full meaning.

Safe channels or perhaps a water hazard will be marked by buoys. How you pass these buoys or how you follow them to another point is the next thing to learn. A buoy is placed and its identifying characteristics are chosen to mark the safe channel as if entering from "seaward." A lot of Skippers remember this rule by memorizing the three R's or *Red Right Returning.* Like this:

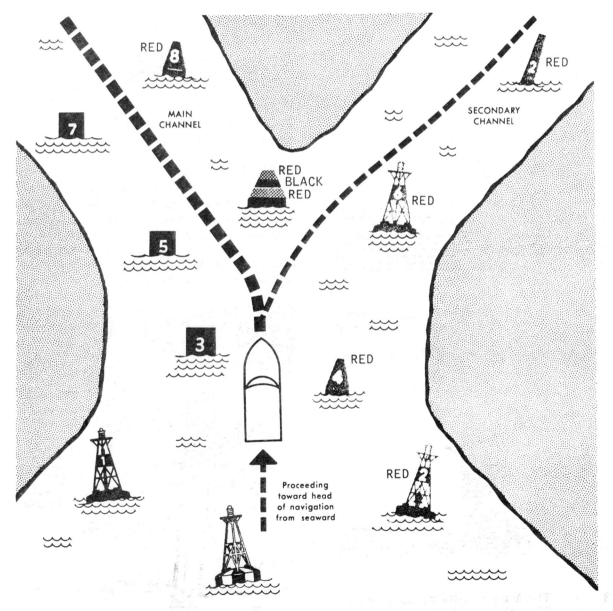

RED
8

RED
2

MAIN CHANNEL

SECONDARY CHANNEL

7

RED
BLACK
RED

RED

5

3

RED
4

Proceeding toward head of navigation from seaward

RED
2

TYPICAL CHANNEL LATERAL BUOY SYSTEM

And of course when leaving port and going out to sea you do the opposite. "Well" you might ask, "what do I do if I'm not entering from seaward?" For boatmen on rivers, going *upstream* against the current is the same as entering from seaward. On lakes when going from the outlet of the lake to its upper end is the same as entering from seaward.

QUICK QUIZ: (Lateral System) (answers on page 64)

In the lateral system of buoys, proceeding in from seaward:
1. Black buoys mark the_____ side of a channel.
2. Red buoys mark the_____ side of a channel.
3. Lighted buoys help you find your way in time of_____.
4. Red-and-black horizontally banded buoys mark_____ in a channel.

A word of caution: Don't regard buoys as immovable objects. They may be missing, drifting, or off their proper position because of storms, tides, and collisions.

Uniform State Waterway Marking System (USWMS)

If you're the kind of Skipper who trailers his boat and rambles around over the highways to various lakes and streams, then this system will be of major interest to you. A lot of water areas used by boatmen are

"I'M ON THE CORNER OF BUZZARDS BAY AND LONG ISLAND SOUND."

located within the boundaries of a state. Since the concept of "proceeding from seaward" or "upstream" cannot be applied, the lateral system cannot be used. The Uniform State Waterway Marking System was devised for this reason and is now used by most states.

First, in the USWMS, buoy *shapes* have no meaning! Second, USWMS buoys come in two categories. A system of REGULATORY markers that tell you of dangerous or controlled areas. The other category of markers are AIDS to NAVIGATION to mark safe channels. These are black and red and are generally used in pairs as in the lateral system.

Regulatory Markers

Regulatory buoys are colored white with international orange horizontal bands completely around the buoy. One band is at the top of the buoy with a second band just above the waterline so that both orange bands are clearly visible.

Different shapes are placed on the white portion of the buoy body and are colored international orange. Shown below are buoys with diamond shapes which always means "BEWARE."

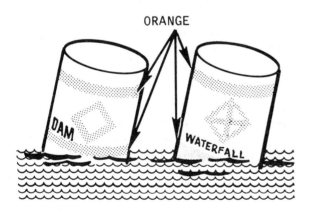

Note the words which are painted on the buoy which describe the hazard to be avoided. This is another advantage for boatmen in the USWMS in that charts are not needed.

In this example a circle is used for the symbol and indicates a control. These can be placed on signboards ashore.

Finally, a square outlined in bright orange gives some form of piloting information. Like this:

Aids to Navigation

Navigational aids used in the USWMS are normally black or red and are used to mark channel limits. Generally they are used in pairs and the safe path is between the two buoys.

Special colored buoys (color) are used where there is no marked channel or where there are scattered underwater dangers. For example:

A white buoy with red top means that a boat must pass to the south or west of the buoy.

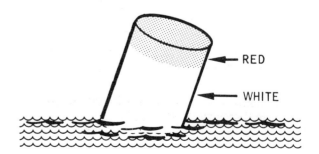

A white buoy with a *black* top means the safe water is to the *north* and *east* of the buoy. Finally, a buoy with vertical red and white stripes marks a danger area between it and shore.

QUICK QUIZ: (USWMS) (answers on page 66)

1. Shown below are examples of the types of buoys used in the USWMS system.

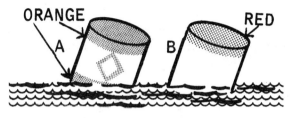

Buoy_____ is an aid to navigation.
Buoy_____ is a regulatory buoy.

2. The shapes of markers used in the USWMS system have no meaning.
   □ a.   True
   □ b.   False

3. When you see this buoy from your boat:

   □ a.   Pass between it and the shore.
   □ b.   Pass outside it and the shore.
   □ c.   Pass on the south or west side.
   □ d.   Pass on the north or east side.

4. Navigation buoys in the USWMS system are generally placed in _____.

5. White buoys with orange stripes and diamond markers mean _____.

6. White buoys or signs with orange stripes and circles mean _____.

7. White buoys or signs with orange stripes and squares mean _____ .

B. Review and Exercise, Part V — Aids to Safe Boating

In this, the final part of your "Skipper's Course" you learned many of the things that will aid you, when operating your boat, to enjoy your cruise and return safely to port. In each of the three main topics, Rules of the Road, navigation lights, and buoy systems, we had the same problem. To cover every possible rule, lights, and buoy is far outside the scope of this program. In each case we chose the rules that would apply to the most readers. Remember, if you desire a more complete coverage of these topics refer to appendices 2 and 4 for the Coast Guard office nearest you and the proper booklet for your specific boating area. Many other useful texts are also listed, and, as always, the Coast Guard Auxiliary, Power Squadron, and State Boating agencies are available for additional information and instruction.

In section B, meeting, crossing, and overtaking situations were discussed using Inland rules of the road. Inland rules of the road are very similar to those rules used in the Great Lakes. In this section you learned the proper signals and actions to be taken for the three most common situations.

In section C, the required lights for boats were covered, again using Inland rules. In this section you taught yourself that the approximate size of a pleasure boat could be determined by its lights. In addition, you learned that you could tell when you were in a meeting, crossing or overtaking situation from the arrangement and appearance of the lights on another boat.

In section D, you learned to identify the meaning of different buoys in the Lateral and Uniform State Waterway Marking System. You also learned the concept of "entering from seaward" so that you would know on which side of your boat to pass a buoy. Just remember "red right returning."

Exercise: Part V
Aids to Navigation (answers on page 68)

In the following situational type problems, you can apply what you have learned about aids to navigation to common boating operation. The problems may involve rules of the road, navigation lights, and buoy systems. In all problems, apply the *inland* rules of the road, and *inland* navigation light requirements.

1. You and your family are on vacation at Florida's Biscayne Bay. You have rented a 32-foot cabin cruiser which is fully equipped to operate on inland waters. Late in the afternoon a small, but fighting mad, Marlin is hooked by the wife and pulled into the boat

"WHEN ARE YOU GOIN' TO FIX THE BELL?"

after a long battle. Heading back in the Snug Harbor Marina you put on your navigation lights and check them. Try to fill in the following blanks without referring to the text. You expect to see the following lights:

a. on the bow a_____ (color) _____ point light, visible for _____ miles.

b. on the right side a _____ (color) _____ point light, visible for _____ mile(s).

c. on the left side a _____ (color) _____ point light, visible for _____ mile(s).

d. on the stern, higher than the bow light, a _____ (color) _____ point light, visible for _____ miles.

2. Maintaining a course that will take you to the channel entrance buoy, you see the white 32-point light of another boat directly ahead of you. No other lights are visible. From the lights you can and can't see, apparently you are in what kind of a rules of the road situation? _____

3. Since the other boat is loafing along in no great hurry, you decide to pass him on his *right* side. To find out if it is safe to do so (being the good Skipper that you are) you sound _____ blast(s) on your horn.

4. Somewhat to your surprise you hear his answer of four (4) short blasts. This is the _____ signal.

5. Apparently he can see something ahead that you can't that would make passing on his right side dangerous. So you decide to propose to pass on his left side and you sound _____ blast(s) (or toot(s) on your horn.

6. The signal you hear him give you back indicates the left side is clear and safe to pass as your hear _____ blast(s) being returned.

7. You ease the throttle up a few notches, turn the wheel to the left, crossing his wake well clear. As you pass him well clear you can now see why his right side was dangerous. You can just make out a small rowboat with someone holding up a _____ light just off the other boat's starboard bow.

8. You're getting close to the entrance channel now as you can see shore lights off both sides of the bow. Then directly ahead you see a quick flashing green light. A quick look with the spotlight shows that it is a black buoy with a number 1 painted on it. According to what your chart says this is the channel entrance buoy and you know it must be passed with the buoy on your _____ side.

9. According to the chart the next buoy is unlighted and should be passed with the buoy on your right side. When close enough to see you note it is the correct buoy because:

a. it is a _____ (shape) buoy.

b. it is painted _____.

c. it has number _____ painted on it.

10. After a week of salt water fishing, skin diving, and boating you travel over the roads to a famous inland fresh water lake for a week of houseboating. (You sure know how to live!) You and the family decide your first trip will be up to the head of the lake to have lunch at a well-known restaurant. Leaving the marina you note that the lake is well marked with buoys in the USWM system. Up ahead just off a point of land you spot a red and white vertical striped buoy. How do you pass this buoy? _____

11. While traveling up the lake you see this buoy. What is the meaning of the symbol?

12. As you near the dock provided by the restaurant, you see a buoy with a speed zone sign on it. What is the shape of the symbol used? _____

ANSWERS: (Navigation) (page 66)

1. a. white 20 2
   b. green 10 1
   c. red 10 1
   d. white 32 2
2. overtaking
3. one (1)
4. danger
5. two (2)
6. two (2)
7. white
8. left
9. a. nun
   b. red
   c. two (2)
10. outside the buoy — never between it and land.
11. Danger or Beware, boats keep out!
12. a circle.

"WELL—YOU DID IT AGAIN."

Now that you have finished the program, you should check your knowledge. Answer the following questions (using the answer sheet on page 75) and mail in the answer sheet for grading. A certificate will be issued if you pass.

1. Flexible tubing used as ducting in boat ventilation systems:
    a. should be at least 15 feet long.
    b. should be at least 2 inches in diameter.
    c. should be at least 20 feet long.
    d. should be at least 4 inches in diameter.

2. A suitable means of backfire flame control must be installed on the carburetor:
    a. of all motorboats.
    b. of all motorboats except those with diesel engines.
    c. all motorboats with gasoline engines.
    d. all motorboats with gasoline engines except those with outboard engines.

3. When aground on mud or sand, you can often get clear by:
    a. immediately shifting to reverse and attempting to back off.
    b. having passengers move and shift their weight.
    c. alternately gunning the engine ahead and reversing in an effort to "rock clear."
    d. determine the point at which the hull is aground, by watching for pivotal motion caused by wind or wave action, shift weight into this point and rapidly alternate weight distribution along a vertical axis.

4. When caught out in foul weather the first thing to do is:
    a. give a proper distress signal.
    b. get everyone into a PFD.
    c. head directly back to port.
    d. drop the anchor.

5. The various buoy systems used are based upon:
   a. The Intracoastal Waterway System.
   b. the Lateral system.
   c. the Uniform State Waterway Marking system.
   d. the Cardinal system.

6. When underway in small open boats, PFD's should be worn by:
   a. children only.
   b. non-swimmers only.
   c. handicapped persons.
   d. everyone.

7. Coast Guard approved hand fire extinguishers for boats may be identified:
   a. by their red color.
   b. by the type of chemicals they contain.
   c. by the stamp on the label.
   d. by the size and weight.

8. Usually, when a boat capsizes, the safest thing to do is:
   a. swim to shore.
   b. make a distress signal.
   c. stay with the boat.
   d. dive under the boat and try to retrieve the cushions.

9. Most fatal accidents involving recreational boats:
   a. are caused by operating at too high a speed.
   b. are caused by careless fueling practices.
   c. are caused by overloading or improper loading.
   d. are caused by operating the boat in bad weather.

10. Under Inland Rules of the Road, when two boats are meeting as shown below, boat A gives the signal:

   a. one blast on the horn to pass port to port.
   b. two blasts on the horn to pass port to port.
   c. one blast on horn to pass starboard to starboard.
   d. four blasts on the horn to pass port to port.

11. Buoys used in the USWM system can be identified:
    a. by red horizontal bands at top and bottom.
    b. by black bands at top and bottom.
    c. by orange horizontal bands at top and bottom.
    d. by their solid orange color.

12. When anchored in a thick fog, under Inland Rules a boat must make an audible fog signal:
    a. every minute.
    b. every two minutes.
    c. every three minutes.
    d. not required by Class A and 1 boats.

13. When *no* fixed fire extinguishing system is installed on Class A or Class I boats with a closed compartment:
    a. one type B-I hand extinguisher must be carried.
    b. one type B-II hand fire extinguisher must be carried.
    c. two type B-I hand fire extinguishers must be carried.
    d. hand fire extinguishers are not required.

14. In the situation below, boat A is said to be:
    a. privileged.
    b. overtaken.
    c. burdened.
    d. not responsible.

15. The international morse code for distress (SOS) can be given on a flashlight or spotlight by:
    a. three long flashes, two short, three long.
    b. three short flashes, one long, three short again.
    c. three short flashes and three short flashes.
    d. three short flashes, three long, and three short again.

16. Portable tanks should be filled:
    a. quickly to avoid spills.
    b. in the forward part of the boat away from the engine.
    c. outside the boat.
    d. from the portable tanks.

17. Large pleasure boats cruising on the high seas must follow the:
    a. Inland Rules.
    b. International Rules.
    c. Great Lakes Rules.
    d. Western River Rules.

18. When approaching a dock against the wind and current, the first line to attach to the dock is:
    a. the stern line.
    b. the forward spring line.
    c. the bow line.
    d. the after spring line.

19. The rules of the road that apply to boats operating on the Mississippi River are:
    a. Inland Rules.
    b. International Rules.
    c. Western Rivers.
    d. Great Lakes.

20. If you are meeting another boat at night head on and the other boat is under twenty-six feet in length, you would expect to see:
    a. one white light.
    b. one green light.
    c. a red and green light with white light
    d. a red light over a green light.

21. In the USWM system, the shape of buoys:
    a. has the same meaning as the Lateral system.
    b. has no meaning.
    c. has the same meaning as the ICW system.
    d. has the same meaning as all other systems.

22. Generally, capacity plates when mounted in a boat:
    a. will be installed by the Coast Guard.
    b. will be installed by each new owner.
    c. will be located near the operator's position.
    d. will be located near the stern.

23. Under Inland Rules of the Road, four short blasts on a horn or whistle means:
    a. intent to turn to port.
    b. intent to turn to starboard.
    c. danger signal.
    d. intent to back out of mooring.

24. When coming up to anchor, the anchor should never be thrown:
    a. because it's too heavy.
    b. because it might foul and fail to dig in.
    c. you might hit another boat with it.
    d. you might damage the anchor cleat.

25. Navigation lights on another boat observed at night:
    a. tell you its course and speed.
    b. tell you it is a class A, 1, 2, or 3 boat.
    c. tell you are meeting, crossing, or overtaking it.
    d. tell you which set of Rules of the Road to apply.

26. When returning the boat to the trailer there should be:
    a. no person in the boat.
    b. one person in the boat.
    c. one person in the boat and one in the car.
    d. one person in the boat, one on the ramp, and one in the car.

27. The daytime signal for small craft warning (winds up to 38 MPH) is:
    a. one red pennant.
    b. two red pennants.
    c. one square red flag with a black center square.
    d. two square red flags with black center squares.

28. The first thing to do when somebody falls overboard is:
    a. yell for help.
    b. speed up the engine and turn back to where the person is in the water.
    c. slow down and turn off the engine.
    d. get something that floats into the water near the person.

29. The most important thing to do at the end of a boat trip is:
    a. plan the next trip.
    b. secure all equipment.
    c. cancel your float plan.
    d. wash down the boat.

30. Returning from seaward, a nun buoy:
    a. marks an obstruction.
    b. marks a channel junction and is solid red.
    c. marks the right side of the channel.
    d. is red with odd numbers.

31. The best time for filling gas tanks is:
    a. when there is a good breeze.
    b. before the sun gets too high and it becomes hot.
    c. anytime in good light.
    d. both a and b are correct.

32. The class of motorboat is determined by:
    a. overall length only.
    b. overall length including outboard engines.
    c. overall length and width.
    d. overall length from rudder to bowsprit.

33. Under Federal law, pleasure craft must be numbered:
    a. based on their class.
    b. based on their overall length.
    c. if capable of propulsion by machinery.
    d. if the motor is 10 horsepower or more.

34. The certificate of numbers must be kept:
    a. on board at all times.
    b. on board when the boat is underway.
    c. in the same place as a car and trailer registration.
    d. on board only when anchored or moored.

35. PFD's must be stored in the boat:
    a. near the bow.
    b. near the stern.
    c. within three feet of all non-swimmers.
    d. where they are readily accessible.

36. Navigation lights on boats are restricted to:
    a. a single color (white).
    b. two colors (red and green).
    c. three colors (red, green, and white).
    d. four colors (red, green, white, and blue).

Directions: Completely cover the letter corresponding to your choice with pen or pencil.

1. a b c d   19. a b c d

2. a b c d   20. a b c d

3. a b c d   21. a b c d

4. a b c d   22. a b c d

5. a b c d   23. a b c d

6. a b c d   24. a b c d

7. a b c d   25. a b c d

8. a b c d   26. a b c d

9. a b c d   27. a b c d

10. a b c d   28. a b c d

11. a b c d   29. a b c d

12. a b c d   30. a b c d

13. a b c d   31. a b c d

14. a b c d   32. a b c d

15. a b c d   33. a b c d

16. a b c d   34. a b c d

17. a b c d   35. a b c d

18. a b c d   36. a b c d

APPENDIX 1 — U.S. COAST GUARD AUXILIARY

The Coast Guard Auxiliary is a volunteer, non-military organization comprised of owners of boats, aircraft and amateur radio stations. Its members receive no pay for their services.

The Auxiliary is established by law to assist the regular Coast Guard in promoting safety and efficiency in the operation of pleasure craft. To accomplish this it carries out three basic programs: Public Instruction, Courtesy Motorboat Examination and Operations.

U.S. COAST GUARD AUXILIARY BOATING INSTRUCTION

The U.S. Coast Guard Auxiliary offers courses in boating safety and seamanship to members of the public. The courses are taught by experienced, qualified Auxiliary members and the only charge is for course materials. Contact your local Auxiliary flotilla or watch for a notice in your newspaper for information. The courses offered are:

Boating Safety and Seamanship (12 lessons) or Basic Seamanship (8 lessons)

These are the Auxiliary's most complete courses. They cover marlinspike seamanship, rules of the road, aids to navigation, piloting, safe motorboat operation and boating laws. Those successfully completing these courses are awarded a certificate by the U.S. Coast Guard Auxiliary.

Principles of Safe Sailing (7 lessons)

Up-to-date complete authorative guide to safely handling today's sailboats in fair weather and foul.

Safe Boating (3 lessons)

A compact and comprehensive presentation of the elements of seamanship and boating is given in this course.

Outboard Motorboat Handling (1 lesson)

This course covers the fundamentals of outboard safety practices, boat handling, equipment requirements and the rules of courtesy afloat.

Basic Boating for Hunters and Fishermen (1 lesson)

This basic course deals with safe boating practices for sportsmen, who account for many boating accidents annually.

THE COURTESY MOTORBOAT EXAMINATION —
A FREE CHECK

Any owner of a pleasure motorboat which is 65 ft. or under can have his boat examined by a specially trained Auxiliary member. Upon the owner's request, the Auxiliarist will make a complete check of the boat's equipment and overall condition to see if it meets all legal requirements, in addition to other Auxiliary safe boating requirements. If the boat passes the examination it is awarded the Auxiliary's official Courtesy Motorboat Examination decal — the seal of safety. If it does not pass, however, the owner is advised of the deficiencies noted. No report of these deficiencies is made to any law enforcement official.

OPERATIONAL ACTIVITIES TO ASSIST THE COAST GUARD

In addition to the voluntary activities in the public instruction and courtesy motorboat examination programs, Auxiliarists participate in the patrol of regattas, and other safety patrols, and in assistance to boatsmen in distress. Auxiliary operations for or with the Coast Guard are always on a voluntary basis.

If you are a U.S. citizen, over 17 years of age and own at least 25% interest in a boat, aircraft or amateur radio station, you may be eligible for membership in the Coast Guard Auxiliary. Special training is given to conditional members so that they may qualify for full membership.

For further information on the Coast Guard Auxiliary and its programs contact the Auxiliary flotilla near you or write the Director of Auxiliary in the Coast Guard District where you live. (See Appendix 2).

OTHER BOATING ORGANIZATIONS

The UNITED STATES POWER SQUADRON has long been active in the promotion of safety afloat through their efforts in boating education. This voluntary, non-government organization, was founded in 1914 and now has some 70,000 members throughout the world. The USPS offers an excellent course on boating to the public. It includes such subjects as piloting, seamanship, and small boat handling. Information on course locations can be obtained by dialing (toll free) 800-243-6000.

The American National Red Cross, YMCA, Boy Scouts, and many States also offer boating courses.

APPENDIX 2

COAST GUARD DISTRICT OFFICES, RESCUE COORDINATION CENTERS and MARINE INSPECTION OFFICES

Office	Address	Telephone	Telephone for Director or Auxiliary
Commander, 1st C.G. District	John F. Kennedy Bldg., Government Center, Boston, Mass. 02203		
Rescue Coordination Center	— do —	223-3645	(617)223-3608
C.G. Marine Inspection Office	447 Commercial St., Boston, Mass. 02109	227-3710 ext. 261	
— do —	76 Pearl St., Portland, Maine 04112	775-3131	
— do —	409 Federal Building, Providence, R.I. 02903	528-4338	
Commander, 2d C.G. District	1520 Market St., St. Louis, Mo. 63103		
Rescue Coordination Center	— do —	622-4604	(314)622-4618
C.G. Marine Inspection Office	— do —	622-4657	
— do —	425 New Post Office Building, Cairo, Ill. 62914		
— do —	301 Post Office & Courthouse Bldg., Dubuque, Iowa	582-7225	
do —	550 Main St., Cincinnati, Ohio 45202	684-3295	
— do —	4th and Chestnut St., Louisville, Ky. 40202	582-5194	
— do —	167 N. Main St., Memphis, Tennessee 38103	534-3556	
— do —	801 Broadway, Nashville, Tenn. 37203	242-5421	
— do —	1215 Park Building, Pittsburgh, Pa. 15222	644-5809	
— do —	5th Avenue at Ninth St., Huntington, W.Va. 25701	529-2524	
Commander, 3rd C.G. District	Governors Island, New York, New York 10004		
Rescue Coordination Center	— do —	422-5700	(212)264-4905
C.G. Marine Inspection Office	— do —	944-4676	
— do —	313 Federal Building, Albany, N.Y. 12207	472-2314	
— do —	312 Post Office Bldg., New London, Conn. 06321	449-7203	
— do —	2d at Chestnut St., Philadelphia, Pa. 19106	597-4350	
Commander, 5th C.G. District	431 Crawford St., Portsmouth, Va. 23750		
Rescue Coordination Center	— do —	393-6081	(703)393-9611 ext. 207
C.G. Marine Inspection Office	— do —	393-6312	
— do —	Customhouse, Baltimore, Maryland 21233	752-2181	
— do —	Customhouse, Wilmington, N.C.	763-9435	
Commander, 7th C.G. District	51 S.W. First Avenue, Miami, Florida 33130		
Rescue Coordination Center	— do —	350-5011	(305)350-5697
C.G. Marine Inspection Office	— do —	350-5691	
— do —	316 Franklin St., Tampa Florida 33601	228-7143	
— do —	210 Federal Bldg., Jacksonville, Florida 32201	354-7555	
— do —	625 Federal Bldg., Charleston, S.C.	747-4171	
— do —	1 East Bay St., Savannah, Georgia 31402	232-4349	
— do —	302 Federal Bldg., San Juan, P.R. 00904	722-2697	
Commander, 8th C.G. District	Customhouse, New Orleans, La. 70130		
Rescue Coordination Center	— do —	527-6225	(504)527-6629
C.G. Marine Inspection Office	423 Canal St., New Orleans, La. 70130	527-6273	
— do —	563 Federal Bldg., Mobile, Alabama 36602	433-3421	
— do —	1601 Proctor Street, Port Arthur, Texas 77641	983-7240	
— do —	232 Customhouse, Galveston, Texas 77550	763-1335	
— do —	101 Federal Bldg., Corpus Christi, Texas 78401	883-5218	
— do —	7300 Wingate St., Houston, Texas 77011	228-4801	
Commander, 9th C.G. District	1240 E. 9th St., Cleveland, Ohio 44199		
Rescue Coordination Center	— do —	861-0400	(216)522-4410
C.G. Marine Inspection Office	1055 East Ninth Street, Cleveland, Ohio 44114	861-0400 ext. 315	
— do —	1212 Ellicott St., Buffalo, N.Y. 14203	842-2000	
— do —	205 Federal Bldg., Oswego, N.Y. 13126	343-6581	
— do —	424 Federal Bldg., Detroit, Michigan 48226	226-7777	
— do —	311 Federal Bldg., Duluth, Minn. 55802	727-6286	
— do —	423 Federal Bldg., Toledo, Ohio 43604	248-7261	
— do —	Municipal Bldg., Saint Ignace, Michigan 49781	39	
— do —	10101 S. Ewing Avenue, Chicago, Illinois 60617	721-3070	
— do —	National Bank Bldg., Ludington, Michigan 49431	843-9135	
— do —	135 W. Wells Street, Milwaukee, Wisconsin 53203	272-3788	

Office	Address	Telephone
Commander, 11th C.G. District	19 Pine Avenue, Long Beach, Calif. 90802	
Rescue Coordination Center	— do —	437-2941
C.G. Marine Inspection Office	750 N. Broad Avenue, Wilmington, Calif. 90744	831-9281
— do —	Broadway Pier, San Diego, Calif. 92101	293-5000
Commander, 12th C.G. District	630 Sansome Street, San Francisco, California 94126	
Rescue Coordination Center	— do —	556-9000
C.G. Marine Inspection Office	— do —	556-5169
Commander, 13th C.G. District	618 Second Avenue, Seattle, Washington 98104	
Rescue Coordination Center	— do —	624-2902
C.G. Marine Inspection Office	— do —	682-1375
— do —	208 S.W. Fifth Avenue, Portland, Oregon 97204	226-3802
Commander, 14th C.G. District	677 Ala Moana Blvd., Honolulu, Hawaii 96813	
Rescue Coordination Center	— do —	50-5888
C.G. Marine Inspection Office	610 Fort Street, Honolulu, Hawaii 96813	
Commander, 17th C.G. District	P.O. Box 3-5000, Juneau, Alaska 99801	
Rescue Coordination Center	— do —	568-2680
C.G. Marine Inspection Office	— do —	586-2680 ext. 20
— do —	P.O. Box 1286, Anchorage, Alaska 99501	

APPENDIX 3

ABAFT   Behind.

ABEAM   Off the side, amidships.

ADRIFT   Not made fast, floating loose.

AFT   At, near, or toward the stern.

AHEAD   In front of the vessel.

AMIDSHIPS   The center of the vessel, with reference to either length or breadth.

ASTERN   Behind the vessel.

ATHWART   Across the vessel's keel line, at right angles.

BALLAST   Heavy material placed in a vessel's bottom for greater stability.

BEACON   A post or buoy placed on a shoal or bank to warn vessels of danger, or to mark a channel. Also, a signal mark on land: a light or radio signal.

BEAM   The greatest breadth of a vessel, also a horizontal support for the deck.

BEARING   The direction of one point or object with respect to another.

BELOW   Beneath the deck.

BILGE   The deepest part of ship's interior.

BINNACLE   A housing located near the ship's helm, containing the compass.

BITTER END   The inboard end of an anchor cable or line.

BITT   A perpendicular post through the deck for securing ropes and cables.

BOW   The forward part of a ship.

BROACH   The turning of a boat parallel to the waves, subjecting it to possible capsizing.

BULKHEAD   A partition or wall.

BULWARK   The side of a vessel extending above the deck.

CAST OFF   To let go a line; as to cast off a bow line.

CHOCK   A fitting to guide a line where it leaves the boat.

CLEAT   A "T" shaped fitting secured to the deck, to which lines are made fast.

COAMING   A raised section around a hatch or cockpit to prevent water from entering.

DECK   Horizontal planking resting on the deck beams of a vessel.

DOCK   A protected water area in which vessels are moored. The term is often used to denote a pier or a wharf.

DRAFT   Vertical distance from the waterline of a vessel to the lowest point of the vessel.

DROGUE   Any device streamed astern to check a vessel's speed, or to keep its stern up to the waves in a following sea.

FATHOM   A unit of length used in measuring water depth. One fathom equals 6 ft.

FENDER   A guard hung over the side of a boat to cushion contact between boat and wharf.

FID   A tapered pin used in splicing.

FLARE   The outward curve of a vessel's sides near the bow.

FOUL   Not clear; jammed.

FREEBOARD   Vertical distance from deck to waterline.

GEAR   A general name for ropes, blocks, tackle and other equipment.

GROUND TACKLE   An anchor and anchoring gear.

GUNWALE   The part of a vessel where hull and deck meet. (Pronounced "gun'l")

HATCH   A covered opening in the deck.

HAWSER   A heavy rope or cable used for various purposes, such as towing or mooring large vessels.

HEAD   A boat's toilet. Also the upper corner of a triangular sail.

HEAVE   To throw, as to heave a line ashore; the rise and fall of a vessel in a seaway.

HEAVE TO   To bring a vessel up in a position where it will maintain little or no headway, usually with the bow into the wind or nearly so.

HEEL   A boat heels when it inclines to one side or the other.

HELM   The machinery by which a vessel is steered, including the rudder.

HULL	The main body of a vessel.
KEDGING	To move a boat in water by hauling on a line attached to an anchor.
KEEL	The backbone of a vessel from which rise the frames, stem, etc.
KNOT	A nautical mile-per-hour measure of a vessel's speed. A nautical mile is approximately 6,076 feet (a land mile, 5,280 feet).
LEE	The side opposite from which the wind blows.
LEEWARD	Direction away from the wind.
LEEWAY	Sideward motion of a boat through the water, due to wind or current.
LIST	The inclination of a vessel to one side.
LOG	A record of courses or operation.
MAYDAY	The international spoken distress signal for radiotelephone.
PAINTER	A short piece of line secured to the bow of a dinghy for towing or making fast.
PIER	A loading platform extending at an angle from the shore.
PLANKING	Boards used for covering the bottom, sides and deck of a vessel.
PORT	The left side of a vessel, looking forward.
PORTLIGHT	A round, hinged window in a ship's cabin.
QUARTER	Either corner of a craft's stern; port quarter, starboard quarter.
RIB	Another term for frame.
SAMSON POST	A single bitt in the bow of a boat, fastened to structural members.
SCOPE	The length of an anchor line, from a vessel's bow to the anchor.
SCUPPER	An opening in a deck or cockpit permitting water to drain overboard.
SEA ANCHOR	Any device used to reduce a boat's drift before the wind.
SHEER	The vertical fore and aft curvature of the deck.
SKEG	A metal extension of the keel for protection of propeller and rudder.
STANCHION	A fixed, upright post used for support.
STARBOARD	The right side of a boat, looking forward.
STEM	The foremost upright timber of a vessel to which the keel and ends of the planks are attached.
STERN	The after end of a vessel.
STRAKE	One line of planks from bow to stern.
SWAMP	To fill with water, but not settle to the bottom.
THWART	A seat or brace extending across a boat.
THWARTSHIPS	At right angles to the fore and aft line. (Athwartships)
TOPSIDES	The sides of a vessel between the waterline and the deck; sometimes referring to onto or above deck.
TRANSOM	The athwartship portion of a hull at the stern.
TRIM	The longitudinal balance of a boat. If either the bow or stern is depressed, the vessel is said to be *trimmed by the bow* or *trimmed by the stern*.
VEER	To change direction.
WAKE	The track or path a ship leaves behind when in motion.
WASH	Waves created by the passage of a moving vessel.
WAY	Movement of a vessel through the water such as headway, sternway, or leeway.
WHARF	Man-made structure bounding the edge of a dock and parallel to the shoreline, for the purpose of loading, unloading, or tying up vessels.
WINDWARD	The direction from which the wind is blowing.
YAW	To swing off course, as when due to the impact of a following sea.

APPENDIX 4 — OTHER USEFUL TEXTS

CHARTS	WHERE TO OBTAIN
Canadian Coast and Great Lakes Waters	Chart Distribution Office Canadian Hydrographic Service 615 Booth St., Ottawa, Canada
United States Coastal Waters	Environmental Science Services Administration U.S. Coast and Geodetic Survey Washington, D.C. 20025
Great Lakes	U.S. Army Engineer District Lake Survey, Corps of Engineers 630 Federal Building Detroit, Michigan 48226
Foreign Waters	Oceanographic Distribution Office U.S. Naval Supply Depot 5801 Tabor Avenue Philadelphia, Pa. 19120
Illinois Waterway (Lake Michigan to Mississippi River) Mississippi River (Cairo, Illinois to Minneapolis, Minnesota)	U.S. Army Engineer District, Chicago Corps of Engineers 219 Dearborn Street Chicago, Illinois 60604
Mississippi (Cairo, Illinois to Gulf of Mexico)	U.S. Army Engineer Corps of Engineers P.O. Box 60 Vicksburg, Mississippi 39181
Ohio River and Tributaries	Corps of Engineers P.O. Box 1159 Cincinnati, Ohio 45201
Tennessee Valley Authority Reservoirs Tennessee River and Tributaries	Tennessee Valley Authority Maps and Engineering Section Knoxville, Tennessee 37900
Marine Weather Services Charts	Superintendent of Documents U.S. Government Printing Office Washington, D.C. 20402
First Aid	Superintendent of Documents U.S. Government Printing Office Washington, D.C. 20402
Magnetic Poles and the Compass	Superintendent of Documents U.S. Government Printing Office Washington, D.C. 20402

COAST GUARD PAMPHLETS   (See Appendix 2)

Rules of the Road:

International — Inland	CG-169
Great Lakes	CG-172
Western Rivers	CG-184
Recreational Boating Guide	CG-340
Emergency Repairs Afloat	CG-151
Marine Communications for the Boating Public	CG-423A
Aids to Marine Navigation of the U.S.	CG-193
Pleasure Craft, Federal Requirements for Boats	CG-290
Marine Emergency and Distress Information Sheet	CG-3892

(Courtesy U.S. Power Squadron)

APPENDIX 5 — FLOAT PLAN (sample)

1. Name of person reporting
   and telephone number

2. Description of boat: Type _____ Color Hull _____
   Trim _____ Ton _____ Registration Number_____
   Length _____ Name _____ Make _____
   Other: _____

3. Persons Aboard _____ Total _____

   NAME   AGE   ADDRESS AND TELEPHONE NO.

   _____   _____
   _____   _____
   _____   _____
   _____   _____

4. Engine Type _____ H.P. _____ Normal Fuel _____ Gals.

5. Survival Equipment: (CHECK AS APPROPRIATE)   Life Jackets   Cushions
   Flares   Mirror   Smoke Signals   Flash Light   Paddles   Food   Water

6. Radio: Yes/No   Frequencies _____ _____ _____ _____ _____

7. Trip: Leave at Time _____ From _____
   Going to _____ or _____
   Expect to return by _____ and in no event later than . . .
   _____.

8. Any other information_____
   _____

9. Automobile license _____ Trailer license _____
   Type _____ Color _____ Make _____

10. If not returned by _____ call the Coast Guard, or
    _____ (local authority), Rescue Center
    _____ (Telephone Number); or _____
    _____ at _____

Notes ...

Notes ...

Notes ...

Notes ...

Notes ...